T0163363

WHAT PEOPLE ARE SAYING ABOUT

HOW TO APPRECIATE AN ARIES

Mary English's books on the signs of the Zodiac provide an ideal way to start learning about Astrology. They are particularly suited to anyone who has had their interest piqued through newspaper Sun-sign columns and wants to learn a bit more. Each book introduces one sign of the Zodiac, and from that basis Mary introduces the reader to the bigger picture – the astrological chart. It seems to me that she strikes a good balance: the basics of constructing a chart are explained, but she never allows this to become dry and theoretical. The reader is kept interested throughout – partly by her lively use of anecdotes, and also because she provides the wherewithal to draw up one's own astrological chart, so that one is learning about Astrology and about oneself from the get-go. Her engaging, conversational style makes the reader feel as if they are having a good gossip with a friend rather than studying, but nonetheless a lot of information is imparted. Her books can be recommended not only to astrological novices, but also to seasoned professionals who feel the need for some astrological refreshment.

Garry Phillipson, author of *Astrology in the Year Zero*

As a double Aries (Sun and Asc), I found Mary English's book, *How to Appreciate an Aries*, a delight. Mary's writing is chatty, accessible and vibrant, and she captures the essence of this sign perfectly. The book is peppered with anecdotes that illustrate vividly Aries characteristics. This is more than just a book on a Sun sign, though, as it introduces the complexity of Astrology in a clear and straightforward way that won't overwhelm the beginner. I'm sure Mary English will inspire her readers to explore Astrology further.

Babs Kirby, author of *21st Century Star Signs* – www.babskirby. com

How to Appreciate an Aries

Real Life Guidance on How to Get Along and Be Friends with the First Sign of the Zodiac

How to Appreciate an Aries

Real Life Guidance on How
to Get Along and Be Friends
with the First Sign of the Zodiac

Mary English

Winchester, UK
Washington, USA

First published by Dodona Books, 2013
Dodona Books is an imprint of John Hunt Publishing Ltd., Laurel House, Station Approach,
Alresford, Hants, SO24 9JH, UK
office1@jhpbooks.net
www.johnhuntpublishing.com
www.dodona-books.com

For distributor details and how to order please visit the 'Ordering' section on our website.

ISBN: 978 1 78279 150 8

A CIP catalogue record for this book is available from the British Library.

Design: Stuart Davies

Printed and bound by CPI Group (UK) Ltd, Croydon, CR0 4YY

We operate a distinctive and ethical publishing philosophy in all
areas of our business, from our global network of authors to
production and worldwide distribution.

CONTENTS

Also by Mary English

6 Easy Steps in Astrology
The Birth Chart of Indigo Children
How to Survive a Pisces (O-Books)
How to Bond with an Aquarius (O-Books)
How to Cheer Up a Capricorn (O-Books)
How to Believe in a Sagittarius (O-Books)
How to Win the Trust of a Scorpio (Dodona Books)
How to Love a Libra (Dodona Books)
How to Soothe a Virgo (Dodona Books)
How to Lavish a Leo (Dodona Books)
How to Care for a Cancer (Dodona Books)
How to Listen to a Gemini (Dodona Books)
How to Satisfy a Taurus (Dodona Books)

This book is dedicated, with appreciation, to the following
Aries ladies:
My friend Mandy: You have always been a tower of strength
Mary: Your feedback, encouragement and support have helped
my writing
Miriam: May you be blessed for being the mother of my
wonderful husband
and
Linda Goodman for being the author of *Linda Goodman's
Sun Signs*

Acknowledgements

I would like to thank the following people:

My son for being the Libran that makes me always look on the other side.

My Taurus husband Jonathan for being the most wonderful man in my world.

Mabel, Jessica and Usha for their homeopathic help and understanding.

Laura for her friendship.

Donna Cunningham for her help and advice.

Judy Hall for her inspiration.

Alois Treindl for being the Pisces that founded the wonderful Astro.com website.

Judy Ramsell Howard at the Bach Centre for her encouragement.

John my publisher for being the person that fought tooth and nail to get this book published and all the staff at O-Books including Stuart, Lee, Nick, Trevor, Kate, Catherine, Mollie, the two Maria's and Mary.

Oksana, Mary and Alum for their read-throughs and welcome additions to the text.

And last but not least my lovely clients for their valued contributions.

Introduction

I am an astrologer and I work in private practice with all sorts of people with all sorts of problems.

I became an astrologer purely by chance. I was trained as a homeopath and one day my homeopath happened to mention that something that I'd said must have happened during my 'Saturn Return' and I thought, 'What the hell is a Saturn Return?'…and I was off. She knew about something, and I didn't, and that in itself was a bit of a challenge.

I was already working in private practice as a homeopath and psychic reader, so it wasn't too much of a diversion to learn about Astrology. And I found it terribly easy. I read books and one of the first I read was *Linda Goodman's Sun Signs*, but it didn't make much sense because I just couldn't identify with her fluffy description of Pisces…so when I found out after further investigation that I had something called a Leo Ascendant and a Gemini Moon, things began to fall into place. I wasn't 'just' a Pisces. I had other 'bits' that made me the person I am.

It was all very exciting.

I then learned about my friends' and family's charts and I got myself a cheap computer programme (that I still use) as it was nice and clear and easy to understand. I like things that are easy to understand. I hate reading books that are written for people with brains the size of universes. They make me lose the will to carry on reading. I prefer to read children's books until I've grasped something, or at least books that have beginners in mind.

I read so many books and made so many charts, I began to see solutions for my clients. I'd 'see' or understand why someone might be finding it hard to get better from an illness because they'd had an awful shock when they were younger, or they were under the influence of some difficult planetary happening.

That made seeing clients a more enjoyable experience. There is nothing worse than treating someone and having no idea if or when they might recover. Or helping a client with a difficult relationship and wondering if they should stay with Mr Not Quite Right or move on to Mr Totally Right.

When I made my ex-husband's chart, I realised what had brought us together, and what had pushed us apart. That was enlightening!

Eventually I was asked by the manager of a local mystical shop if I'd come and read palms in her premises, so I ended up with a buy-two-get-one-free approach of card readings, palm readings and Astrology all in one reading.

At first I kept my Astrology clients and Homeopathy clients apart, and rarely mentioned one to the other. Now I use both in my practice to good effect.

After a while I began to see a lot of Pisces in my practice and, since I'm a (reformed) Pisces myself, I thought I'd write a guide-book called *How to Survive a Pisces* to help my clients understand our sign better. But my publisher, who amazingly is a Pisces, told me he wouldn't accept just one book from me, so I thought I'd do one for each sign...and it was then that I realised I'd got a rather big project on my hands: 12 books!

It had taken me over 2 years to write the first one and find a publisher; now I was going to be writing 11 more books. Argh! Then my publisher sold the foreign rights to a Brazilian publisher to be translated into Portuguese and they wanted all 12 books within a certain time-limit. Argh again!

As I'd started at the end of the Zodiac, I thought I'd go backwards (why not??!) and so here we are at the first sign of the Zodiac – Aries – and my last book in the series.

So I have taken a week off work and checked myself into a retreat in Radstock in Somerset to complete the series in time for spring 2013. I hope I manage to pull this off!

And that's a bit like the Aries energy. They won't say 'No'. It's not a word that's in their vocabulary. They try lots of seemingly difficult tasks, with relish. They certainly like a challenge, and getting 22,000 words (I've got 3 other books to complete this week) written in 5 days is certainly a challenge!

So, I hope you enjoy reading and learning about the sign of Aries, the first sign of the Zodiac.

Mary English

Bath, 2013

Chapter One

The Sign

As a kid, I always was obsessed with Houdini.
David Blaine (both Houdini and David Blaine are Aries)

Assertive, honest, impatient. These three qualities are attributed to Aries the Ram, the first sign of the Zodiac in Astrology.

So what is a sign of the Zodiac?

What is Astrology?

Where and why did Aries get its name and what do people think about Aries today?

All these questions and more will be answered in this little book.

I learned a little about Aries while researching this book. Originally I'd decided to call it *How to Tackle an Aries* but one of my (very nice) newsletter subscribers objected (quite rightly) to this rather outdated and unfair portrayal of her character type. To tackle an Aries suggests they are a type of person who is always on the lookout for a fight. It's a boxing term. It's also a fishing term as tackle is what you take along to catch fish.

So Mary (as that is also this lady's name) and I had an exchange of emails:

> **How to Tackle an Aries!!! Mary, please, not that!** *It has the connotation of bringing us to our knees! Bringing us down...Which, of course, is a favorite pastime of many people.*
>
> *And right now I'm feeling flattened; so that title is just the last thing I want to see! Non-Aries people may rejoice at the title, but I can't imagine any Aries being happy with it. I know the word 'tackle' has other connotations; but I sure don't like it one little bit!*
>
> *Is it not possible to 'Admire an Aries'??? Accept an Aries? Live*

in Accord with an Aries? Adapt to an Aries? Analyze an Aries? Anchor an Aries? Coexist with an Aries? Appeal to an Aries? Appraise an Aries?

How to Appreciate an Aries *would be nice. That gives you plenty of room to list all of our negative aspects as well as how to deal with them.*

Mary

Me:

Hi Mary,
I'm glad you replied.

I was worried about the title, which is why I sent the titles in the email...will develop a new one and get back to you :)

Mary xx

Mary:

Thank you! I'm sure you'll come up with something clever.

M

Me:

How to Anchor an Aries?

Mary xx

Mary:

Not bad; but would you really want to tie us down??? It did sound OK to me at first, but we are pretty independent.

*Again, it's one of those words that can be taken two ways – we do need grounding/anchoring (at least I do, since I'm mostly Fire and Air); but **tying us down** – anchoring us to a pier/post or in the middle of the sea – would be anathema! You do want us to be out*

5

there exploring, pioneering, and blazing trails, don't you? ;-)
Why don't you like 'Appreciate'?
Mary

Me:

Oh I missed 'Appreciate'…I will give that some thought; good idea! I am working on this today!
Speak soon,
Mary xxx

Me:

What would you want people to know the most about Aries?…Where has the misunderstanding mostly affected you?

Mary:

We may be blunt, but we mean no harm.

Me:

'Appreciate' is good but sounds a bit Leo…like all an Aries wants is praise.
What about 'Accept'?
You've suggested that already and I'm beginning to like it…if more people accepted the way Aries are, exploring, pioneering, trail-blazing…wouldn't that make it easier for an Aries to feel happier?
Hmm…'Accept' is beginning to sound nice…what do you think?
Mary xx

Mary:

'Accept' is OK, but not terribly catchy. God knows, acceptance would be a blessing, however!

I guess I still prefer 'Appreciate', which is much different than 'Admire', which is more Leonian. We certainly do not look for praise, but I think we would like our unique talents and abilities to be appreciated (recognized) in spite of our obvious drawbacks.

How about 'Understand'? How to Understand an Aries.

Mary

Me:

'Appreciate'…checked with hubbie – his mum was Aries.

'Appreciate' it is!

Thank you Mary xxx, very helpful xxx

This exchange of emails, I hasten to add, occurred not when I'd started writing the book, but a few days before I finished it, and was off to the retreat to complete the writing of it. This is where Aries strength lies. They don't waste energy on something that isn't needed NOW, this very moment in time…

As you can see from the above exchange, Mary didn't release her grasp from her idea until she was sure I had grasped what she wanted me to know. As the exchange went further, she stopped signing her name, didn't begin her email with mine…she just GOT TO THE POINT…and it's this that can startle other signs of the Zodiac: Aries' ability to be so blunt! But Mary was blunt for a *reason*. This was her sign that she was talking about. Her moniker. Her flesh and blood.

People can be very protective of their sign of the Zodiac, even people who don't follow Astrology much.

So, there we have it. *How to Appreciate an Aries.*

Don't need to write the book now, do I? You've completely

understood what 'appreciate' is all about.

No?

Let's get a little perspective on Astrology itself before we get further into understanding this sign.

So what is Astrology? As Nicholas Campion says: 'Astrology's character descriptions constitute the world's oldest psychological model...which remains the most widely known form of personality analysis.'

This is very true. We use Astrology to describe people's personalities, not just make predictions. I don't actually do much predicting in my practice; I mostly do E.F.A: Emotional First Aid.

Astrology began a long, long time ago, more than 2,000 years. It's even mentioned in the Bible – remember the Three Wise Men? They were following a star...

A Very Brief History of Astrology

Christopher McIntosh, a historian, tells us in his *Man, Myth and Magic: Astrology*:

In Babylonia, where Astrology began, astrological knowledge was regarded as an important part of a man's education. It was said, for example, as proof of the indolence of King Ninus that 'he saw no star, nor seeing it took note'.

The less educated classes worshipped the stars in a cruder way, looking on them as deities, but everyone was familiar with the planetary and constellation figures...

Babylonian astrology was, at first, used only to predict general events such as natural disasters, wars, rebellions and the like. But about the time of Alexander's conquest of that area (4th century BC), individual horoscopes began to be cast.[1]

Eventually Astrology made its way, by word of mouth, across the oceans to Greece, Egypt, Rome in Italy, and then to the rest of Europe, changing little in meaning and delivery in that time. The symbols we use today are still the same universal symbols, so that people from all walks of life can understand them, and you will too.

Early astrologers had to be able to read and write and calculate difficult mathematical placements of the planets, something that computers now do easily. You won't have to do anything difficult to make the birth charts we're going to make in this book.

I'd like to make a few distinctions about what Astrology is, and isn't. A lot of people seem to think that Astrology is all about prediction. As if all astrologers do all day is look 'into the future'. This is not entirely true. There are all sorts of astrologers, just as there are all sorts of people.

Some astrologers are interested in the history of Astrology; some involve themselves in counselling, or business advice, or Sun-sign columns in the media, or personality profiling. Some are interested in psychology, health, relationships or politics, but all, mostly, are interested in the 'whys' of life and the reasons. They are interested in the *meaning* of life.

Basic Principles

When we talk about Sun signs, what we mean is the sign that the Sun (that big ball of flames) was in on the day the person was born. And when we say 'sign' all we mean is the portion of the sky we've denoted to 'be' that sign of the Zodiac. Just like I live in the county of Bath and NE Somerset, while you might live in New York, NY. The signs of the Zodiac are simply divisions of the sky above us. Nothing more, nothing less.

And Astrology isn't just about the Sun. Along with the Moon and the Sun there are at least nine other celestial bodies in the sky that we observe and plot their paths as they orbit around the Sun: Mercury, Venus, Mars, Jupiter, Saturn and the three more recent discoveries of Uranus, Neptune and Pluto which I discussed in my books *How to Bond with an Aquarius*, *How to*

Survive a Pisces and *How to Win the Trust of a Scorpio* respectively.

Astrology and astronomy were once the same science but they've now parted company. We still use astronomical data to calculate a birth chart, but the difference between astronomers and us is the *meaning* behind those planetary placements.

The Study of the Planets, Not the Stars

Astrology is the study of the planets. Not the stars. The stars just hang in the sky millions of miles away. They don't orbit around our Sun, and they are visible all year round from Earth. Not in the same places because, don't forget, the Earth moves on its axis, so at different times of year, different parts of the Earth are facing into different parts of space.

The planets are in our neighbourhood and orbit around the same Sun as us. If we were to make a little map of those planets on the day you were born, that would be what we call a 'horoscope', or 'birth chart' or, as they call it in America, a 'natal chart'.

So there we are, orbiting around the Sun. All day, every day.

And all these other planets in our solar system are doing the same thing. Not at the same time, or the same distance or even the same speed, but for the last gazillion years and a few more gazillion to go, we will be orbiting the Sun.

Now the early astrologers didn't know that we orbited the Sun. All they knew was what they could *see*, which is the Sun making its way across a thing called the 'ecliptic path' every day, and as they plotted it, they saw that at certain times of the year it was in different places. They thought, quite understandably, that the Sun orbited around the Earth, because at night it isn't visible...where has it gone? They weren't daft. They knew the Sun and the other planets would appear again...but when?

That's when the early astronomer/astrologer Babylonians plotted the paths of the bits they could see in their clear night skies. They saw that only certain blobs in the sky moved. Some were always there, like the Polaris star or Pegasus...but blobs like Venus came and went.

They also came to the conclusion that there must be a connection between these heavenly bodies and our life here on Earth. And why wouldn't it be so? We're all part of the same universe. All living in the same bit of space. Surely there must be some sort of connection between us?

Neighbourhood Watch

It's a bit like neighbours. You might be like most people, never visiting or talking to your neighbours, getting on with your life, sure in the knowledge that they're doing their thing and you're doing yours. But what if you found out their names, and what they did for a living?...Maybe they could help you if you have a flood when your washing machine breaks down, or you could use their freezer when yours conks out, or when they're going away on holiday you could feed their budgie/cat/hamster/rabbit.

It's like that in the universe. It doesn't necessarily make our lives any better knowing our neighbours, but if we noticed that every time we had a hurricane, Mars was in Gemini, we might pay more attention.

That's the basic principle of Astrology. An awareness of our neighbours and an understanding that we're not alone in the universe, and those planetary bodies are our friends.

Our Cosmic Fingerprint

So a horoscope is a bit like a fingerprint; it tells us about ourselves and our potential.

So what is an Aries? An Aries is a person who is born when the Sun was in the bit of the sky we've called 'Aries'. And that bit of the sky (from our view on Earth) is determined by the spring solstice. That happens generally around 21st March and, as there are 12 signs of the Zodiac, we divide the year up into 12 equal portions, and the Aries portion lasts until 20th April.

However, just to make things difficult, it does depend on where in the world you were born and at what time of day. If your Aries was born at 2am on 21st March, they might still be a Pisces, so we're going to use a nice reliable website to give us the correct and accurate information.

Each sign of the Zodiac has a planet that 'looks after it'. We call it their 'ruler'. The ruler to Aries is Mars, the God of War.

The Astronomy of Mars

The surface of Mars is covered with a layer of iron oxide or rust, which makes it look red from our view on Earth. It is often called 'the red planet' and most resembles Earth even though it is a lot smaller, just 4,222 miles in diameter.

Unlike the Moon, Mars' surface is weathered by winds and its desert surface has seasonal dust storms. Various probes have been sent to the surface over the years and have discovered channels and gulleys which appear to have been sculpted by running water.

Like the Earth, Mars has seasons and weather and it takes just over 24 hours to rotate once on its axis. However, it takes 687 days to orbit the Sun, which is longer than our year of 365 days.[2]

During a winter on Mars, a third of its atmosphere can remain frozen above the polar ice caps. It also bears the scars of a heavy bombardment of meteoroids that formed impact craters and basins.

It was first viewed by the USA's 'Mariner 4' in 1965; then again between 1971 and 1972 'Mariner 9' viewed the planet. In 1976 the US spacecraft 'Viking' descended to its surface but produced inconclusive results. During the 1990s the Mars 'Pathfinder' landed in the Valley of Ares, which is rather fitting as a name!

Since then, further information has been recorded about its atmosphere, rock surface and weather conditions.

Mars is also host to two moons named Phobos and Deimos after two of Ares' sons, according to Greek mythology.

The best time to observe Mars is when it is in opposition to (opposite) the Sun and closest to Earth. During this alignment of Mars, the Earth and the Sun, which takes place every 26 months, Mars' red glow can be seen with the naked eye.[3]

Mars in Astrology

Mars is the red planet, the colour of blood and emotion and, not surprisingly perhaps, the God of War to the ancients. If Venus is the archetypal girlie of the solar system, Mars is the original lad, standing for ambition, competitiveness, willpower and the active pursuit of the attractive.

Mars was the Roman God of War, and the planet Mars symbolizes our aggressive nature. The appearance of the planet Mars, in its fiery red colour, suggests action. We also tend to hear it being referred to as 'the angry red planet' and other such terms. Mars represents how we go about getting the things we want, how we assert ourselves and express our independence, and also how we defend ourselves when we are under attack. Mars is the complement to Venus, and both have to do with the mechanics of desire and attraction.

Mars also represents our courage, determination, and freedom of spontaneous impulse. People ruled by Mars are noticeably ambitious, positive and fond of leadership. They are quite inventive and mechanical and can become good designers, builders and managers, and usually make their way to the front of whatever they undertake.

Words that are related to Mars are the name of the month March, the name of the planet Mars (hence the Martians), martial law and martial arts.

Now don't just take my word for it. I'm not the first astrologer to write about the Sun signs.

The Best-Selling Astrological Author

Someone who wrote only about the Sun signs (not the other

planets or how to make a chart) and who managed to get her book *Linda Goodman's Sun Signs* onto the *New York Times* Best Sellers List with over one million copies sold by 1976 was, as the name suggests, a lady called Linda Goodman.

Linda was an Aries, so we can be sure that her description of her sign is accurate, as writing about what you know is easier when you're actually living it:

Have you recently met an unusually friendly person with a forceful manner, a firm handshake and an instant smile? Get ready for a dizzy dash around the mulberry bush. You've just been adopted by an Aries. Especially if you found it a little tough to take the lead in the conversation.

Is he committed to some idealistic cause and angrily defending the underdog? That figures. Male or female, these people will fight what they feel is injustice on the spot, and they're not bashful about voicing their opinions. The ram will talk back to a traffic cop or an armed gangster with equal vigour; if either one happens to annoy him. He might regret it later, but caution won't concern him in the heat of the moment. Mars people come straight to the point, with no shilly-shallying.

Let's ask a few other astrologers for their views on Aries.

Here's Colin Evans in his *The New Waite's Compendium of Natal Astrology* in 1967:

Aries individuals are characterised by intellectuality, self-reliance, activity, energy and impulsiveness. They are pioneers in the realms of thought and action, though they are more idealistic than practical. Always wilful and headstrong when young, most of them fail to achieve the necessary measure of caution even in mature life and continue to go to extremes.[4]

Hmm, sounds as if Colin's Aries are cowboys herding wild animals...Let's ask Marion and Joan in their *The Only Way to Learn Astrology* in 1981:

> 'I am'
> - Pioneering, executive, competitive, impulsive, eager, independent, dynamic, lives in present, quick...domineering, quick-tempered, violent, hasty, arrogant, 'me first', brusque, lacks follow-through.[5]

These are some of the Aries characteristics, but I actually know some Aries who are quiet and rather shy...

Let's see what Felix Lyle and Bryan Aspland say in their *The Instant Astrologer* in 1998:

> Assertive, wilful, independent, self-centred, enthusiastic, impatient, honest, reckless, competitive, argumentative, energetic, decisive, domineering, passionate.[6]

Caroline Casey, in true Libra style, paints a slightly more balanced view in her *Making the Gods Work for You* in 1998:

> Aries people appear to be independent, yet because they seek their identity through others, their secret, as revealed by the opposite sign of socially self-conscious Libra, is that no sign cares more deeply about relationship. They prefer any kind of interaction – even negative – to none at all: 'If we can be friends, that's great; if not, let's fight.' Combat is a form of intimacy. If they cannot get anyone else to fight with them, they will provoke a fight with themselves.[7]

Hmm, again there seems to be this fixation with fighting. As if all Aries are dressed to kill (literally) with a gun or spear in hand...

Let's ask Bil Tierney in his *All Around the Zodiac* in 2001:

Full Speed Ahead.

Of all the signs of the zodiac, Aries seems to be the most desirous of speed. Fire and air signs appreciate quick responses in life, but being cardinal and fire, Aries demands the fastest results and can be quite impatient when time seems to drag.[8]

This is very true; I've seen this speed first-hand...

Gina Lake, in her *Symbols of the Soul*, discusses the more esoteric qualities of this sign in 2011:

They have an unshakable belief in themselves and in their ability to deal with life, bolstered by an underlying sense of justice and rightness about the world.[9]

This sounds more like the Aries I have met and know.

OK, that's the writers. Let's ask a few Aries *themselves* about their sign's attributes.

Cathy is a self-employed therapist, living and working in a big bustling city in the UK:

'Just saw your message, and thought I'd like to add a passing thought: that, as an Aries passing through life and seeming to cross every hurdle as if it's the first each time, could it be easier being another star sign?

'Seems that brushing oneself off and starting all over again with optimism, time and time again, is a trait one becomes accustomed to, and in the words of Scarlet O'Hara in Gone With the Wind (I believe she was another Aries): "...tomorrow is another day."'

Yes, this does describe the Aries trait of not giving up on themselves or their views.

Margaret is a full-time mother and life coach. She told me a bit about her sign:

'Aries can be stubborn! My father, myself, and my daughter are all Aries. Aries truly are natural born leaders! Stubborn they may be, but yes, they are sensitive too. This allows them to be not so stubborn that they can't also be understanding, which just makes them better leaders! Of course, I'm biased, being an Aries myself.'

Some people are really happy about their Sun sign. Jessica works as a section leader in a call centre:

'I first heard of Astrology through reading the star-sign columns of newspapers as a child. I loved that I was born an Aries. It really captured my imagination that – at some soul-deep level – I was a warrioress like She-ra (my favourite cartoon).'

Even though most people know about their Sun sign, not everyone finds out about the other bits of their chart. Like me, Penelope found out her Rising sign (Ascendant) and it changed her life:

'My Aries Sun sign was all I knew about Astrology for years. Nobody else in my family is interested in Astrology – I'm self-taught. When I grew older I learned from the Internet that I was a Scorpio Rising, and that explained some more things. In the past, when I had been part of "Guess my Star sign" conversations, people always thought I was a Scorpio. And now, knowing my Rising sign, I finally know why! I've been learning about Astrology as a hobby ever since.'

A few word-qualities are repeating themselves here: Independent/Leadership, Hasty/Impatient, Enthusiastic, Wilful, Courageous/Brave and Assertive.

Independent/Leadership
Mandy is a retired teacher living in Chicago and mother to four

children. She tells us about her leadership skills:

'I am and always have been a leader. I'm the oldest child and the only girl in my birth family. I'm a retired teacher – the benevolent dictator in my classroom. In my Aries innocence I sometimes go where angels fear to tread.'

I asked Leander, a pharmacy clerk for a health authority, 'How much of a leader are you?'

'Although I've been more of a hermit lately, my leadership qualities are improving. Inside this shy girl is someone who wants to show and teach others how they can overcome extreme adversities and learn to feel good about themselves, share my experiences and show them how they can help themselves to not only survive, but thrive.'

'How do you feel when you have to take orders, or instructions, from someone?'

'In the past, very frustrated. Not any more – I don't take instructions from anyone, unless I agree to it first. If I don't agree, I just leave the situation. Well, recently, with my elderly mother, I was checking the electrical wires on the outside of the lift chair when it wasn't working. She had to tell me every step. I got frustrated, because at 59 years old, I think I can look at a few wires to see if they are plugged in or not, and I told her so, not screaming or anything. Just letting her know she could stop it. Then I dropped it and went to the other side of the room and sat down.'

'What drives you crazy?'

'People telling me what to do. Loud-pitched noises. People who won't take no for an answer and try to argue with me until I say yes.'

Poppy is a housewife, mother, widow and alternative therapist. She used to work as a legal secretary. She tells us about her leadership skills:

> 'Yes, I guess you could call me a leader. I like to organise and sort things out and I like to bring people together for their highest good, i.e. be a facilitator.
>
> 'I have no problem taking orders or instructions from someone – I have been employed in that situation and had no problem. But if it is something new I am doing – like when I was learning to drive I would ask my instructor to tell me once and then let me work it out for myself – I have to be able to use my "brain" and not be bottle-fed! I was always chosen to "train" new employees when I worked in an office. Aries – and I am describing ME – are loyal, protective, impatient, emotional, independent, strong and hard-working leaders; I will always rise to a challenge!'

This love of independence is experienced not just with people in the modern world; it's been happening for a long time.

Isambard Kingdom Brunel was born in 1806 and is a rather famous person where I live. He commissioned the construction of the Clifton Suspension Bridge, an immense undertaking at that time. He said: 'I am opposed to the laying down of rules or conditions to be observed in the construction of bridges lest the progress of improvement tomorrow might be embarrassed or shackled by recording or registering as law the prejudices or errors of today.'

Notice that key word in the above quote: 'shackled'. That would be an Aries' biggest fear: to be held back, or tied down by others, preventing free expression of their objectives and ambitions.

The quickest way to disempower an Aries is to hold them back from being involved in something they feel deeply about, that they know they can do, that they have dreamt about, thought about, planned and practised...I'm sure you get my drift.

It says on his Wikipedia page, 'Though Brunel's projects were not always successful, they often contained innovative solutions to long-standing engineering problems.'

This doesn't matter to an Aries. They don't mind making mistakes (especially if they have Sagittarius planets) and will just continue on, regardless of opposition. In fact if you want an Aries to do something, tell them NOT to do it! That will add fuel to their flame...

Hasty/Impatient

My worst quality is impatience.
Emma Thompson

Karen is a massage therapist and a single mother to two young daughters. She lives near me in the West Country.

'I am very impatient. I'm just no good at waiting for anything, so I guess waiting makes me cross...especially for people who are late! Also people who faff around, people who are slow and indecisive!'

Elaine has a degree in counselling and lives in Indiana, USA, with her dog Rum. She tells us about her impatience:

'It varies, depending on how stressed I am. Mostly, quite impatient, and I've been given feedback about it several times.'

'What makes you cross?'

'When I feel like my time is being taken up by too many requests from the same person. Also being told how to do something I already know how to do. And the big one: being criticized. When others put me in their "box", not caring to know who I really am.'

Poppy tells us about her impatience levels:

'Very impatient! To the point of having a strop!'

Courageous/Brave

I'm a hero with coward's legs.
Spike Milligan

One thing that defines an Aries is their ability to go boldly where others might think twice. When an Aries has a project on the go, or an idea they're chasing, it would be very hard to reduce their drive. Aries won't worry about 'what others think' if they're convinced that what they are doing has merit.

Aries writer, poet, black spokesperson and rape survivor Maya Angelou has never shown any fear in speaking her truth. She tells us: 'One isn't necessarily born with courage, but one is born with potential. Without courage, we cannot practice any other virtue with consistency. We can't be kind, true, merciful, generous, or honest.'

Samuel Hahnemann, the 'inventor' of Homeopathy, whose chart we will be exploring, met plenty of opposition to his new ideas. But since he was motivated by a desire to bring healing to medicine rather than sickness, and to not join his contemporaries in their drastic medical applications, he can easily be thought of as courageous. It does take courage to go against mainstream thinking, dogma, or current trends.

Sometimes the Aries desire to win at all costs could be seen as foolhardy. There is less likelihood of discussion or negotiation; these are more Libra qualities. As Aries singer Marvin Gaye says:

'Negotiating means getting the best of your opponent.'

Validation

I wrote an article that I posted on my website in the late 1990s about Indigo Children's birth charts. It was the result of five years' research into their birth-chart shape which is unique in that so many of them are born with one-sided charts with Uranus and Neptune conjunct.

An Indigo is a person born to challenge authority's way of making us all do the same thing, but without a good reason. They are a race of people that are here to 'change how we do things', and not always in acceptable ways. The recent imprisoning of three Russian women, the so-called 'Pussy Riot', is an example of Indigos not really negotiating well. They had a point; they just went about it in a more challenging way.

My article drew a lot of visitors – so far it's in the 25,000s – and I occasionally make a few observations and comments on the website www.indigosociety.com.

One of the young men I 'met' on there was an Aries. He was so taken away with the whole Indigo concept and my astrological observations – which were that a race of people were born with very distinct birth charts, with all their planets on one side of the circle and Uranus and Neptune very close together; this only happens every 170+ years – that he made a YouTube video of my research.

The reason I am mentioning this is because that young man was an Aries...and one of the key things he said in his YouTube video was:

'I met Mary and she validated me.'

He wanted me to validate his existence as an Indigo.

So what is 'validation' to an Aries?

My dictionary defines 'validate' as: 'to check or prove the validity or accuracy of. Demonstrate or support the truth or value of'.

And what is 'valid'? 'Actually supporting the intended point or claim. Its origins are from the late 16th century French word *valide* or Latin *validus*, meaning "be strong"'.

Putting this into easy English: It means an Aries wants to be supported in what they do and who they are. To be recognised for their strength of spirit, which actually must take a certain amount of personal energy to maintain. As Aries Abraham Maslow said: 'We may define therapy as a search for value.'

Chapter Two

How to Make a Chart

It really is very easy to make a chart these days. You don't have to calculate difficult angles or degrees, or work out the latitude or longitude of the place of birth. You also don't have to worry about 'Summer Time' or 'War Time' or any other time.

All you need is three pieces of information and access to the Internet.

First off you need:

- The date
- The time
- The location of your Aries' birth. Something like 31st March, 4pm, London, England.

To make your Aries' chart, go to www.astro.com and make an account; then go to the 'Free Horoscopes' section and scroll down and use the special part of their site, called the 'Extended Chart Selection'.

You've already inputted all your data, which will be shown in the box at the top where your name is.

Scroll down the page again, and under the section marked 'Options' you'll see a box that says 'House System' and in the box it will say 'default'.

Now make sure you *change the box to say* 'equal'. The default system is called Placidus and all the houses will be different sizes, and for a beginner that's just too confusing.

We're going to make the chart of Samuel Hahnemann, the founder of Homeopathy, a form of alternative medicine. He was born 'shortly before midnight' on Thursday, 10th April 1755.*

You will see a picture of Samuel's chart at the start of Chapter

Three. The lines in the centre of the chart are either easy or challenging mathematical associations between each planet in the chart, but for our purposes, ignore them.

The houses are numbered 1–12 in an anti-clockwise order. We will be learning about them in Chapter Five.

We only want 3 pieces of information: the sign of the **Ascendant**, the sign the **Moon** is in, and the **house** number that the Sun is in.

This is the abbreviation for the Ascendant: AC, which we will learn about in Chapter Three.

This is the symbol for the Sun, which we learned about in Chapter One: ☉

This is the symbol for the Moon, which we will learn about in Chapter Four: ☽

These are the shapes representing the signs, so find the one that matches yours. They are called 'glyphs'. The symbol for Aries looks like the letter V, sort of like the horns of the Ram.

Aries ♈
Taurus ♉
Gemini ♊
Cancer ♋
Leo ♌
Virgo ♍
Libra ♎
Scorpio ♏
Sagittarius ♐
Capricorn ♑
Aquarius ♒
Pisces ♓

The Elements

To understand your Aries fully, you must take into account which element their Ascendant and Moon are in.

Each sign of the Zodiac has been given an element that it operates under: Earth, Air, Fire, and Water. I like to think of them as operating at different 'speeds'.

The **Earth** signs are **Taurus, Virgo** and **Capricorn**. The Earth element is stable, grounded and concerned with practical matters. An Aries with a lot of Earth in their chart works best at a very slow, steady speed. (I refer to these in the text as 'Earthy'.)

The **Air** signs are **Gemini, Libra** and **Aquarius** (who is the 'Water-carrier', *not* a Water sign). The Air element enjoys ideas, concepts and thoughts. It operates at a faster speed than Earth, not as fast as Fire but faster than Water and Earth. Imagine them as being medium speed.

The **Fire** signs are our friend **Aries, Leo** and **Sagittarius**. The Fire element likes action and excitement, and can be very impatient. Their speed is *very* fast. (I refer to these as Firey i.e. Fire-sign.)

The **Water** signs are **Cancer, Scorpio** and **Pisces**. The Water element involves feelings, impressions, hunches and intuition. They operate faster than Earth but not as fast as Air. A sort of slow-medium speed.

Chapter Three

The Ascendant

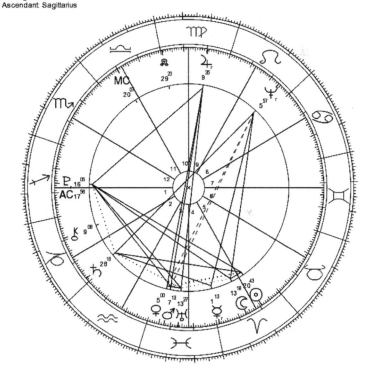

In our chart example above, we see the chart of Samuel Hahnemann, the originator of Homeopathy.

Now, whether or not you agree that Homeopathy is a valid form of medicine (I think it is, but then I'm biased – I'm trained in it myself), Hahnemann was a pioneer in his day as he vehemently disagreed with the barbaric practices that his medical peers were involved in.

'Medicine' included body purging, massive enemas, violent laxatives or nauseating emetics to induce vomiting. Blood-sucking leeches were applied to the body, sometimes as many as sixty, and blood letting was also carried out, all in the name of health and healing. 'These were the seeds of Hahnemann's discontent and subsequent rebellion. The inhumanity, the barbarism and the quackery of medical practice in his day appalled him.'[10]

Now, if you've made Hahnemann's chart correctly, you'll see the initials AC at the ¼ to position in the segment of the chart numbered 1.

And the sign symbol around the outside of the chart that looks like an arrow – that's the symbol for Sagittarius.

Try not to let all the symbols put you off. They're only shorthand for astrological information. They're not there to confuse you or make Astrology difficult. They are there so that Astrology can be understood by anyone from any country in the world.

So, Samuel has a Sagittarius Ascendant. What does that mean?

Well, we know that Samuel is an Aries because he was born between the dates when the Sun is usually in the part of the sky we've called Aries: March 21st – April 20th.

But on the day he was born, at that particular time, the sign of the sky that was rising (Ascending) at just before midnight was...Sagittarius.

This doesn't stop him being an Aries. It adds to his Aries character. And boy, did it add!

Sagittarius is the sign of long-distance travel, further education and philosophy. Samuel certainly travelled. He was born in Meissen in Saxony, then lived in:

Leipzig
Hettstedt
Dessau

Gommern
Dresden
Lockwitz
‑Leipzig (again)
Stotteritz
Gotha
Georgenthal
Molschleben
Pyrmont
Hamburg
Mulhausen
Gottingen
Brunswick
Wolfenbuttel
Konigslutter
Altona
St Jurgen
Molln
Machern
Eilenburg
Wittenburg
Dessau (again)
Pfarrgasse-Torgau
Leipzig (again)
Kothen
Lastly Paris, where he died aged 89 in July 1843.

Since travel in those days was by horse and cart, and a journey to Paris from Kothen would take 14 days at least, we can tell this is a man who's not *afraid* to travel.

Aries is fearless and Sagittarius loves to travel.

The Ascendant describes 'how' you came into the world. The specs you wear, the coat you have, the outside part of you that people 'meet' first. It's the way you tackle life.

If your Ascendant is Taurus, you might have come into the world more slowly, in a more patient way. If your Ascendant is Scorpio, maybe there was extreme emotion in your birth; maybe your mother risked life and death.

The Ascendant tells us how someone starts a project (not finishes it) and approaches his or her life. Some astrologers call the Ascendant the 'Life Path' and tell us it describes the road we will walk along.

It doesn't change your innate self = your Sun sign, but it does modify how it is expressed.

So here are all the Ascendants that an Aries can have.

Check the chart you've made for yourself or your family member/friend and read how that Ascendant affects their Aries-ness.

Does it add to it?

Or detract?

Or slow it down?

Or speed it up?

Aries Ascendant

Gay guys love women who are tough, who are survivors. I've pulled through everything and I've not become bitter about it.
Samantha Fox

An Aries with an Aries Ascendant (or Moon) is 110% Aries. So all those fearless, fighting-spirit, hasty words are expressed with blatant honesty and lack of finesse. No one or nothing is going to tell them what to do, where to do it, or why it should be done. They've already worked this out and are aiming their focused gaze on the next exciting project.

Taurus Ascendant

Looking at beautiful things is what makes me the happiest.
Ali MacGraw

Ruled by Venus the Goddess of Lurve, Taurus Ascendant wants to surround themselves with all that beauty and goodness can bring. A full stomach, or at the very least a full larder, enough money to enjoy the nicer things in life, and a much slower pace compared to their Sun. Routines, practical actions and a need to enjoy their experience of life.

Gemini Ascendant

The camera can photograph thought.
Dirk Bogarde

The light, flighty Gemini Ascendant energy gives an Aries an even quicker thought-process. Ping! Pong! Another thought goes racing through their minds. Always on the alert for something happening and fun, they rarely rest and certainly don't settle. They might move house, change job, ditch one idea for another, but their life certainly won't be boring.

Cancer Ascendant

It's a fenced-in part of the yard and there's a little house at the back which we built for the dogs to sleep in at night.
Emmylou Harris

The most empathic Water sign, Cancer Ascendant gives a more emotional exterior to the upbeat Aries Sun. The family, including lost kittens and homeless puppies, will be the centre of their attention and nothing is more enjoyable to them than being surrounded by those they love. It doesn't matter if their relatives have blood ties, as long as they are part of 'the family'.

Leo Ascendant

I don't know if the camera likes me, but I do like the camera.
Celine Dion

Leo loves to shine. They also, as a fellow Fire sign, give an Aries the ability to shine even when it looks as if today will be a rainy day. The eternal optimist meets the friendly lion and rejoices when they are praised, sulks when they are ignored. They gaily dash in where angels fear to tread, or rarely explore, and can swiftly change a tragedy or mishap into a full dramatic production.

Virgo Ascendant

How can anybody hate nurses? Nobody hates nurses. The only time you hate a nurse is when they're giving you an enema.
Warren Beatty

Virgo is concerned with health, healing and keeping the body healthy, sparkly and in good physical shape. The ability of this Ascendant to give Aries some grasp of attention to detail is a plus. It can also quite cleverly disguise their true nature and make them seem a little meek and mild. This is an illusion. They're still the leader; they just prefer to be the *perfect* leader.

Libra Ascendant

I'm always looking for meaningful one-night stands.
Dudley Moore

To unite with 'The One' is the siren cry of Libra Ascendant, which is slightly at odds with the Aries need to attend to the 'I' or 'Myself'. This is an eternal battle of wits and one that is won only when the Aries bits allow their significant other to share their personal space. Then they learn that it is possible to love someone and be loved in return without losing autonomy.

Scorpio Ascendant

We think too much and feel too little.
Charlie Chaplin

Intensity, passion and strong willpower go well with the Aries psyche. This can incline the person to be a bit too intense, a bit too independent and self-actualised, but nonetheless this is a strong Ascendant to have. They are the emotional survivor and the last one to admit defeat when the stakes are high. Their X-ray eyes look deep into your soul, and 'trust' is their key word.

Sagittarius Ascendant

Every man's life is a fairy tale written by God's fingers.
Hans Christian Andersen

Aiming their arrows of discovery high into the sky, Sagittarius Ascendant for an Aries brings a searching, curious attitude that never seems to be satisfied. They love international relations, exploring other cultures and their beliefs, and if they think they're right, no amount of discussion or argument will make them change their mind.

Capricorn Ascendant

He exploited all of the young people who worked for him, but he really gave you responsibility and opportunity. So it was kind of a fair deal.
Francis Ford Coppola

Ruled by severe Saturn, the God of restraint and fiscal responsibility, their life-view revolves around that which has to be worked hard for. They are ambitious and forward-focused and their fear is lack of resources and/or money. Consequently when they've worked out where they are going, nothing will stand in their way and, like a climber, not a comet, they will reach that highest point.

Aquarius Ascendant

The weirdest thing that has happened has been my discovery that people who attend the conventions are filled with love.
William Shatner

This is a more zany and weird Ascendant for an Aries to have and, ruled by the 'wacky planet' Uranus, heralds someone who wants to 'be different'. They also yearn for freedom and hate instruction, orders, rules and regulations and anything that holds them back from exploring. More focused on groups rather than individuals, and definitely altruistic. They will save 'the world', and yours too.

Pisces Ascendant

We are eternally linked not just to each other but to our environment.
Herbie Hancock

Fairies, soft angels singing, connecting with the cosmos and the expanses of creation appeal to this Ascendant. Fuzzy thinking and tardiness can be the result. They love the esoteric and that which can't be explained. They can sense someone's hurt from 50 paces and will do anything to prevent further suffering. Ruled by Neptune the Water God, splashing about with emotions and feelings will be high on the agenda.

Chapter Four

The Moon

If the Sun represents our 'Ego' or bigger self, then the Moon in Astrology represents exactly what she is in real life: the reflection of the light from the Sun.

This is the anima to the animus.

The conscious to the subconscious.

The thought vs. the emotion.

For centuries the Moon has been worshipped as the bringer of the feminine, the Goddess of feeling, the light in the darkness. She doesn't have any light of her own and takes it from the Sun's eternal rays. The Sun gives; the Moon receives. Keep these ideas in mind when you read about the various Moons in their signs, as they're slightly different from the Sun signs. While the Aries Sun will get up and go, the Aries Moon will get het-up and go. (There's a subtle difference.)

To find out the Moon sign of your Aries, look for the Moon symbol ☽ in their chart. In our example chart, Samuel had his Moon in the sign of Sagittarius.

I have only covered here the signs the Moon can be in, not where their location in the chart might be. This is because this is a little introductory book. If you want further information about the placements of your Moon in the chart, please either contact me, or go back to astro.com and you'll find a free analysis under the tab 'Free Horoscopes'.

The Dr Bach Flower Essences

In 1933 Dr Edward Bach, a medical doctor and homeopath, published a little booklet called *The Twelve Healers and Other Remedies*. His theory was that if the emotional component a person was suffering from was removed, their 'illness' would also disappear. I tend to agree with this kind of thinking as most illnesses (except being hit by a bus) are preceded by an unhappy event or an emotional disruption that then sets into place the body getting out of sync.

Removing the emotional issue and bringing a bit of order into someone's life, when they are having a hard time, can improve their overall health so much that wellness resumes.

Knowing which Bach Flower Essence can help certain worries and upsetments gives you and your Aries more control over your lives. I recommend the Essences a lot in my practice if I feel a certain part of a person's chart is under stress, and usually it's the Moon that needs help. The Essences describe the negative aspects of the character, which are focused on during treatment. This awareness helps reverse those trends, so when our emotional selves are nice and comfortable, we can then face each day with more strength.

I've quoted Dr Bach's actual words for each sign.

To use the Essences take 2 drops from the stock bottle and put it into a glass of water and sip. I tend to recommend putting them into a small water bottle, and sipping them throughout the day, at least 4 times. For young children, do the same.

Remember to seek medical attention if symptoms don't get better and/or seek professional assistance.

Aries Moon

For some reason, I seem to be bothered whenever I see acts of injustice and assaults on people's civil liberties. I imagine what I write in the future will follow in that vein. Whether it's fiction or non-fiction.
Iris Chang

The exuberant, assertive Aries Moon's feelings, like their Sun's, are expressed powerfully and impetuously. Their gut reaction to events is honest and there is no doubt that what they feel is genuinely 'in the moment'. Being a more speedy sign, their emotions are like the storm, swift to occur and just as swiftly to pass away.

Bach Flower Essence Impatiens: *'Those who are quick in thought and action and who wish all things to be done without hesitation or delay.'*

Taurus Moon

He leads the way back into the kitchen, sits down at the table and offers tea and biscuits. *'I've got good dunking ones,'* he laughs. *'Specially flown in from France.'*
Elton John

A Taurus Moon, for an Aries, slows things down a little, and makes them more likely to want to indulge in good food and tactile contact. They are emotionally consistent and slow to change their heart. They also love all of life's tastier offerings including fine wine, chocolates and luxury treats.

Bach Flower Essence Gentian: *'Those who are easily discouraged. They may be progressing well in the affairs of their daily life, but any small delay or hindrance to progress causes doubt and soon disheartens them.'*

Gemini Moon

I'm a hero with coward's legs.
Spike Milligan

With airy, abstract Gemini energy being the prism through which they experience their emotions, an Aries with this Moon is more likely to analyse their emotions. The plus side of this is the clarity of their self-knowledge; the minus is that they may end up simply worrying about it all too much. Sometimes the answer to their emotional problems may be to simply turn their brain off for a while.

Bach Flower Essence Cerato: *'Those who have not sufficient confidence in themselves to make their own decisions.'*

Cancer Moon

You can't be a great mum and work the whole time.
Emma Thompson

This brings a double portion of lunar influence, for with the Moon in Cancer it is in its own zodiacal home. The emotions are well tuned into protecting and nurturing others and maternal matters rate highly. The risk is that they may find themselves too sympathetic and can consequently feel overwhelmed by all the sorrows in the world. Emotional protection is a necessity.

Bach Flower Essence Clematis: *'Living in the hopes of happier times, when their ideals may come true.'*

Leo Moon

Find a place where there's joy, and the joy will burn out the pain.
Joseph Campbell

Leo's traditional love of being in the limelight means that Moon-in-Leo people are likely to have an instinct for being the centre of attention. They are happiest with an appreciative audience, oodles of praise and the archetypical red-carpet treatment. Lavish them with praise and affection and they will gently purr with appreciation.

Bach Flower Essence Vervain: *'Those with fixed principles and ideas, which they are confident are right.'*

Virgo Moon

I am a very reclusive, private person.
Camille Paglia

Virgo Moons are often seen as somewhat problematic – the Virgoan emphasis on order and harmony can sit uncomfortably with our notoriously uncontrollable emotions. As Virgo is a mutable sign it can mean their emotions will be fluid and hard to define. For an Aries this can bring a personal difficulty in wanting action laced with definition. Provided they are given time to 'work things out their own way', they're happy.

Bach Flower Essence Centaury: *'Their good nature leads them to do more than their own share of work and they may neglect their own mission in life.'*

Libra Moon

If you find it in your heart to care for somebody else, you will have succeeded.
Maya Angelou

Libran energy puts a strong emphasis on harmony and balance and gives the Moon-in-Libra person a refined aesthetic awareness, naturally good instincts or 'taste'. Slightly trickier is the question of relations with others. The fear of expressing emotions which will cause difficult scenes means that Moon-Librans may say one thing while secretly feeling (and hence, doing) another. As this is the opposite sign to their Sun sign, they might occasionally think one thing, and do something else...if they can make up their mind.

Bach Flower Essence Scleranthus: *'Those who suffer from being unable to decide between two things, first one seeming right then the other.'*

Scorpio Moon

I am the only performer who ever pledged his assistants to secrecy, honor and allegiance under a notarial oath.
Harry Houdini

Scorpio is notoriously associated with murky depths, deep longings, deep passions and deep feelings. There is no doubt they feel things strongly and passionately. As a fixed sign, they will also not change their feelings often. On the plus side this produces a character that is not afraid of fear, which coupled with the Aries Sun, makes someone who might not take 'No' for an answer. On the downside it can cause paranoia and suspicion.

Bach Flower Essence Chicory: *'They are continually correcting what they consider wrong and enjoy doing so.'*

Sagittarius Moon

It is better to be high-spirited, even though one makes more mistakes, than to be narrow-minded and all too prudent.
Vincent Van Gogh

With the Moon in Sagittarius, their emotions are ruled by upbeat, benevolent Jupiter and this gives a trusting and positive outlook on life and people. Moon-in-Sagittarians always bounce back and never lose their faith in humanity. They can shoot their emotional arrows in the air, confident that they will hit the target eventually. However, this can produce a situation where they end up making the same mistake again and again. Best to think first, act later.

This Essence comes under the heading 'Over-Sensitive to Influences and Ideas'.

Bach Flower Essence Agrimony: *'They hide their cares behind their humour and jesting and try to bear their trials with cheerfulness.'*

Capricorn Moon

If we don't succeed, we run the risk of failure.
Al Gore

Capricorn is the sign concerned with the tough material reality of the world and, ruled by stern Saturn, can make for someone who is overly serious. They might take a bleaker attitude to how they feel, or be overly critical of their emotions. On a bad day, life looks grey. On a good day they have the determination to succeed where others might give up, and gain steely nerves in the process.

Bach Flower Essence Mimulus: *'Fear of worldly things, illness, pain, accident, poverty, of dark, of being alone, of misfortune. They secretly bear their dread and do not speak freely of it to others.'*

Aquarius Moon

If I decide to be an idiot, then I'll be an idiot on my own accord.
Johannes Sebastian Bach

An Aries with Moon in Aquarius might find their emotions hard to get to grips with. Aquarian energy is airy and gives a natural tendency to distance themselves from their feelings, or to consider them in an abstract way. They are very unlikely to wear their heart on their sleeve, and people may find them cool and unpredictable. However, freedom is important to them so they won't worry about what you think.

Bach Flower Essence Water Violet: *'For those who like to be alone, very independent, capable and self-reliant. They are aloof and go their own way.'*

Pisces Moon

I tell kids to pursue their basketball dreams, but I tell them to not let that be their only dream.
Kareem Abdul-Jabbar

Pisces is *the* most emotional of the signs, and with the Moon here, an Aries will have extreme emotional sensitivity. They have an awareness of suffering and a desire to connect with spiritual insight, a love of fairies, angels, mysticism and all forms of divination. More than others, they need time alone to re-configure when stressed and dreaming is important to them.

Bach Flower Essence Rock Rose: *'For cases where there even appears no hope or when the person is very frightened or terrified.'*

Chapter Five

The Houses

It is a little more difficult to explain what a 'house' is if you haven't actually ever made a birth chart. It's only when you make more than one chart that you realise that all the different bits end up in different places. Those different places are what we call the 'houses'. They used to be called 'mansions' as they are 'home' for each planet.

In our example chart, Samuel has his Sun in the 5th house.

This is calculated by the computer programme. If he was born a couple of hours earlier his Sun would fall into the 4th house and so on. The further into the day you're born, the further clockwise round the wheel of the chart your planet lands up.

I was born at 4pm in the afternoon, so my Sun sign of Pisces is in the 7th house. If I'd been born at 6am, it would be in the first house.

So the house placement is determined by the time of birth. Nothing else. Just the time.

You can check a chart is correct by imagining that the horizontal line going from left to right, dissecting the chart, is the horizon. So if your Aries was born during the day, their Sun *should* be located above the horizon in the upper part of the chart...as the Sun would be overhead.

If they were born at night, when the Sun went down, their Sun should be in one of the houses below the horizon, as obviously, the Sun had 'gone down' at the time of birth.

Don't worry about this too much if it doesn't make any sense, as all you really need to know is that their Sun could be in any one of the 12 houses. Provided you've made your chart using the correct time, the Sun will 'be' in the correct house. And as there are 12 houses, it could be in any one of them.

Look for the ☉ symbol in the chart that you have made and see which numbered section it has ended up in; then read the description below.

You will, obviously, only need to read the description that relates to the chart you have made.

So what is the *meaning* of having the Sun in different placements? Well, we think of each house as being a bit like each sign of the Zodiac. So the first house is a little like the sign of Aries, and so on. Having the Sun in the first house is totally different from having it in the 7th house, as the first is all about 'the self' and the 7th is all about 'others'.

The placement of the Sun modifies its expression. It doesn't change 'who' that person is; they're still motivated by all those Aries qualities we've discussed already, but they express them differently.

This is where having your own personal birth-chart made up makes Astrology totally individual to you. As there are 12 houses, and we're just using the Sun's location (in a full chart you'd be taking into account at least 8 other planets and the Moon AND making sense of it all!!), we're keeping it as easy as possible.

As I mentioned, my Sun is in the sign of Pisces in the 7th house, but my mother (whom I wrote about in *How to Bond with an Aquarius*) has her Sun in the sign of Aquarius, in the 9th. We've both got Moon in Gemini, so we both love to yak, but where we 'are' in life is different.

Where your Sun is located is where you feel 'at home'. Where you like to spend your life focus the most.

If your Sun is in the 3rd, you'll like writing or chatting or teaching or anything associated with the 3rd house, but if your husband or significant other has their Sun in the 8th, they're going to want to keep a bit of themselves secret and will like to get deeply involved in feelings.

There is more than one 'house system'. I use Equal House but most people use Placidus, so unless you make your chart using the Equal House system my interpretations won't be the same. I must point out that there is no agreement among astrologers as to what is the 'correct' system. You have to find the one you like the most.

The First House: House of Personality

We live at the edge of the world, so we live on the edge. Kiwis will always sacrifice money and security for adventure and challenge.
Lucy Lawless

This is a highly significant Sun position, since it means that they were born very near the dawn. It gives a nice warm, sunny outlook on life and one that is swifter and good at action. As a Sun-dominated chart, it helps someone be more confident, more self-assured and capable of acting swiftly and with confidence.

The Second House: House of Money, Material Possessions and Self-Worth

Captain Kirk has been a source of pleasure and income for a long time.
William Shatner

With the Aries Sun in the second house, there will be an earthy materiality in the basic character. This can typically be expressed as taking pride and pleasure in possessions. Venus rules this house, so the combination of pleasure in materiality and earthy sensuality means they could be quite attracted by luxury and indulgence, and will certainly value that which can be bought and held in their hands.

The Third House: House of Communication and Short Journeys

One way I find meaning in life is through the belief that we all have a deeper Self or core Self which guides, unfolds and regulates our growth and development.
Howard Sasportas

The mind and communication are featured in this placement. This can make them a natural communicator and thinker, possibly quite intellectual. Development of the mind is likely to be important and maybe higher academic studies of some sort. The Mercurial input here (Mercury being the ruler of the house) also features travel and mobility, so they are happiest poodling along the highways and byways of life.

The Fourth House: House of Home, Family and Roots

The important point which I keep stressing is that it is impossible to try to imagine the future unless you understand the past.
Dane Rudhyar

The Aries Sun in the fourth house lays emphasis on roots, security and family, and an understanding of the relationship with parents, and the mother in particular (since this house is ruled by the Moon, the eternal mother). They will be family-oriented in some way and this may find expression in less obvious ways – by treating friends or work colleagues as though they are part of a big family. The past is also important.

The Fifth House: House of Creativity and Romance

With an eye made quiet by the power of harmony, and the deep power of joy, we see into the life of things.
William Wordsworth

This is a happy placement, since the fifth house is the home of creativity and romance. Being the centre of attention is also a plus. Red carpets, heaps of praise and appreciative recognition keeps the Sun in this house happy. Being artistic and creative, or giving birth to children or good ideas are all expressed here.

The Sixth House: House of Work and Health

In the landscape of extinction, precision is next to godliness.
Samuel Beckett

The sixth house has its focus on everything related to health. It also is the work that we do. The Aries Sun here will want to be well, healthy and organised. It's also not unheard of for them to work in the health and healing sector or, at the very least, to be concerned with their own and others' health. Less likely to be sloppy or wishy-washy.

The Seventh House: House of Relationships and Marriage

Marriage requires a special talent, like acting. Monogamy requires genius.
Warren Beatty

The Aries Sun here will want to share their life with another significant other. Being single won't wash. Until their close personal relationship is organised life feels bleak. When attached life has new meaning. There will be a strong desire to unite 'as one', which might conflict with the Aries desire to 'lead'. They feel best with a ring on their finger and 'The One' near at hand.

The Eighth House: House of Life Force in Birth, Sex, Death and Afterlife

You have first of all to side with your own spirit, and your own taste. Then take the time, and have the courage, to express all your thoughts on the subject at hand. Finally you have to say everything simply, not striving for charm, but conviction.
Francis Ponge

The Sun in the eighth house feels things deeply. The intensity of this house with the Aries Sun makes an individual who is strong in character and un-swayed from their life's mission. Boredom is not on the menu! The ability to focus exclusively on one thing at a time can bring great results. Life and death are experienced as periods of transition.

The Ninth House: House of Philosophy and Long-Distance Travel

When I have a terrible need of – shall I say the word – religion, then I go out and paint the stars.
Vincent Van Gogh

Provided that the ninth house Sun in Aries can philosophise about life's true meaning all is well. Foreign countries, long journeys, and an interest in other cultures will be expressed here. This house is associated with travel – the further, the better – and with 'knowledge', be that spiritual, scientific or philosophical. They enjoy all sorts of cultures and love to travel mentally and physically. Keep passports at the ready.

The Tenth House: House of Social Identity and Career

It is our responsibilities, not ourselves, that we should take seriously.
Peter Ustinov

Sun in the tenth wants to make their mark on the world. They will be motivated to influence as many people as they can to reach their Nirvana, wherever or however that might manifest. As Saturn rules this house, they might progress more slowly but with determined deliberation they will reach whatever heights they set their mind to.

The Eleventh House: House of Social Life and Friendships

I'm not a do-gooder. It embarrassed me to be classified as a humanitarian. I simply take part in activities that I believe in.
Gregory Peck

With the Sun in eleventh an Aries will have fairly extensive social connections, and will like mixing with others. This enjoyment in people may also be blended with altruistic motives of some sort, by enjoying charitable work or similar. They could have a humanitarian, humane character, finding pleasure in social groups that benefit others. More likely to avoid the intimacy of close relationships.

The Twelfth House: House of Spirituality

Sometimes I would almost rather have people take away years of my life than take away a moment.
Pearl Bailey

Having the Sun in the twelfth house implies a sensitive, dreamy and secluded side. They are more likely to be at their best working behind the scenes, out of the limelight. However, provided they can have this seclusion occasionally, they can reach spiritual heights and mystical union.

Chapter Six

The Difficulties

There's a line in the picture where he snarls, 'Nobody tells me what to do.' That's exactly how I've felt all my life.
Marlon Brando

Now that we have learned a little about the Aries psyche and how to make a birth chart, we're now going to learn how to overcome any difficulties you might come across with the Aries in your life. This is by no means an exhaustive list, but it does cover a few key circumstances that you might find difficult to solve.

These are the sorts of things I hear in my private practice, as my clients don't come and see me when their lives are going well.

No, appointments are made when lives fall apart, tragedies happen, mix-ups occur and conflict is experienced.

Having over 30 years of experience helps me advise my clients with practical answers and workable solutions.

'I'm getting tired! I can't keep up! My Aries is rushing me from here to there!'

This is, I'm afraid, a common complaint by people who misunderstand Aries. If you're a fellow Fire sign of Leo or Sagittarius, this might not bother you much, as you are already running around, doing this, arranging that, going here today and there tomorrow.

If you're an Air sign – Gemini, Libra or Aquarius – you're more likely to be able to keep up and if you run out of steam you're more likely to tell your Aries you're tired. You might even have a 'discussion' about it.

But if you're a Water or more especially an Earth sign, you're going to get too exhausted to even complain. And when you do complain, it will all come out wrong...

There is only one way to deal with this.

You are going to have to be completely honest and say, 'I would prefer to slow down. I'll catch you up later.'

You can't travel at the Aries speed, so don't try. You might have an accident.

One of my sisters dated an Aries gentleman. Most of the time, he was just that: a gentleman. Until one bright and sunny day, when we were visited by a long-lost relative, from Texas in America, who was a truck-driver.

And this person not only drove a truck, but was a *female* truck-driver.

Alarm bells started to ring in my head when the introductions were over, as I could see we were going to be in for some 'competition'.

Mr Aries got it into his head that he was 'going to show' Ms Truck-Driver that no woman was ever going to be a better driver than him. In the house he was as mild and as nice as can be, but the minute he got behind the steering wheel, with Ms Truck-Driver at his side, he sped off down the road at a fair old pace. 'Oh, dear,' I thought, as my life flashed in front of my eyes, 'I'd better check that my safety belt works' (which it did, luckily).

We then reached a rather hilly part of Bath, and Mr Aries took off down the hill into the countryside at about 60 miles an hour. The speed limit was 50 and I was praying we'd get stopped by the police. Ms Truck-Driver was as calm and cool as a cucumber, but Mr Aries was flinging the steering wheel around, and the car was swerving round the corners as we went down the hill because it was a very bendy road.

My sister and I were sitting in the back of the car and, just while I was working out how to say something to get him to slow down, my sister gave me one of those 'Don't interfere!' looks...and we arrived at our destination.

Although we'd gone out for lunch, I now really wasn't in the mood for eating...

I found out later that Ms Truck-Driver is a Scorpio, which was why she was so cool about him driving like a lunatic.

Never again. From that day forward, I drove myself wherever we needed to go...I'm a Water sign.

Diane Lang, a blogger, has this to say about Aries and speed. She's a balanced Libra:

'I have Aries on the brain and just want to relate some things I'm seeing happen to the Aries folk in my extended family. The intense Aries influence seems to manifest not only with intensity but FAST!

'My husband was born under a sky filled with planets in Aries. He has Sun, Moon, Mercury and Jupiter in Aries, along with an early Aries Rising.

'Last weekend we visited our Aries Moon granddaughter who had a "cold". My husband started showing symptoms on Tuesday, lost his voice on Wednesday, went to bed early on Wednesday evening with a slight fever, slept until noon on Thursday, and is now back working again. He let the fever run its course and burn out the virus...a very Aries thing to do.'

Another of my sisters has been with her Aries sweetheart since they were 13. She has Aries Moon; he has an Aries Sun. A marriage made in heaven!

Except sadly they will never marry as they both have Down's syndrome and my sister is terminally ill with dementia.

When he was little, Master Aries was into trains, and used to skip out of the house and down to the station – no fear at all – to see his favourite trains. He would climb over walls, run around the garden and get up to all sorts of tricks, which would drive his Virgo mother into meltdown. I wish I'd known about Astrology then; I might have been able to offer some solutions.

'My Aries wants us to get married yesterday; tomorrow isn't soon enough.'

If this is happening to you, I do offer a few words of caution. While it's good for an Aries to speed their way through most of their life, speeding into marriage is generally a recipe for disaster.

Your Aries might love you truly, madly and deeply, but unless they've seen you cut your nails, or brush your teeth, or look unkempt at 8am in your pyjamas, they will just as swiftly go off you and be back into the dating game again.

This is the one time when a little application of the brakes on the relationships will do the world of good. And to slow down also, in these types of circumstances, is the best solution and I will explain why.

To keep your Aries waiting for love is a GOOD THING. Your Aries needs to work for your love, not have it handed to them on a plate, all done and dusted.

No.

They will feel better if they have to cross miles of rivers and seas to find you, travel over mountains and streams, drive thousands of miles across the outback or desert to win your love.

They won't want it to be found at the bottom of the garden, or right there in their living room. Unless they have a number of planets in Cancer, your average Aries will enjoy the challenge of *winning* your love. And this applies as equally to males as it does to females.

An Aries woman who has decided you're going to be her life partner, come hell or high water, will stop at nothing to have her desires met. And the more challenging this is, the more she will want it.

I have a little story to share. A chap I know was born into a devout Catholic family, and this son of the family started dating his sweetheart when they were studying at university. A few years passed and they moved into accommodation together.

Then Ms Aries decided that son-and-heir was going to be her beau, and she announced her engagement. Well, they both announced it, but Ms Aries also told *all* of her family, so there was no going back.

Son-and-heir's father was mortified. Son-and-heir was the only boy in his family and the only son, who would inherit the family's Catholic-ness...except Ms Aries was a confirmed atheist.

Father objected. Strongly. Regularly: 'No son of mine is going to marry someone who isn't a Catholic.'

Battles lines were drawn. Meetings were planned. Father made long car journeys to dissuade son-and-heir from marrying his sweetheart.

Ms Aries stood firm.

The marriage happened. No one backed down and, years later, now that various older members of their respective families have died, it seems unimportant in the telling of it.

The point is, Ms Aries *didn't* back down.

She stood her ground, and no amount of persuasion otherwise would have made her change her mind. And more than four decades later I almost think that she would have dumped son-and-heir if his family had agreed 110% to the union and welcomed her with open arms. The challenge would not have existed and the 'spoils' of 'war' would have felt less satisfying.

'Help! My Aries hates their/my mother, father, sister, brother, cousin, boss, next-door neighbour...and it's making our/my/their life hell.'

Are you sure it's hate? Maybe it's more that your Aries doesn't like something they are 'doing', not something they are 'being'.

Aries rarely object to people just because of a temperament or personality defect. If their values, or actions or ideals aren't in line with their own, that's where the trouble starts. So you'll have to reassess the situation.

Has the relative/friend/neighbour said/done anything that's

against your Aries' view of life?

Remember what we were discussing earlier about Aries wanting validation for their existence. Does this person agree or disagree with your Aries over some point you may have overlooked?

Have you looked at it from their point of view?

You might have to become the balanced/fair Libran in all of this, but I can guarantee, your Aries will want to be 'right' and the other side will want to also. It's more a question of ideas rather than personhood.

Equally, were your relative/friend/neighbour to be under attack from some *other* party, your Aries would be likely to fight for your cause, rather than continue to oppose them.

As Karen, the therapist we met earlier, loves to say:

'Don't forget this saying of mine – and of my Aries dad: "We have many faults, but being wrong is not one of them."'

Just accept that your Aries isn't wrong, neither is the relative/ friend/neighbour, and try and make sure you don't add fuel to the fire by challenging your Aries. This is one time in your life when ignoring the whole situation will work best. Ignoring it will remove the fire from the situation and make your Aries less likely to continue to be at war.

'My Aries has an awful temper. Should I say anything?'

This depends on a) what sign you are, and b) if you have a temper too.

There can't be agreement here. EITHER you *tell* them (not ask them) to reduce their outbursts or you're off. OR you agree to only get worked-up in certain circumstances, and stick to your agreement.

Aries actress Emma Thompson admits to having a temper:

'But when I lose my temper, I find it difficult to forgive myself. I feel I've failed. I can be calm in a crisis, in the face of death or things that hurt badly. I don't get hysterical, which may be masochistic of me.'

You will find this trait in most Aries. In a crisis, they will be cool and in control, but if they lose their car keys, or can't get through on the phone or are kept waiting in line for too long, they will get cross.

If your Aries has a terrible temper, and you're finding that difficult to live with, find out what their Moon sign is; then follow the Moon's monthly cycle and, on 'their' Moon days, which will be over two days every month, either be out of range or out of the house, or at the very least out of sync with them.

If they kick off, tell them then that unless they calm down RIGHT NOW (not later or tomorrow, as the feelings will all have blown over by then), you will leave and **never come back**.

And you will have to stand your ground firmly and mean what you say; otherwise your Aries will tune into your lack of resolve and carry on tormenting you.

Be firm!

'My Aries is leading a new project and wants my support, but from where I'm sitting it looks like it's all going to end unfavourably.'

If your Aries wants to 'do' something, don't even waste your precious life-energy by disagreeing.

Poppy tells us what makes her excited and raring to go:

'Probably a new challenge, something different, learning something different, helping someone with something they are struggling with – I just have to get involved!'

And there's the key word: 'challenge'. Aries enjoys a good challenge. Don't take that away from them.

Not every Aries wants total commitment from everyone in their life, but what they do want is your support. And you can frame it like this:

You don't think, in your humble opinion, that this project / new career / marketing / selling / relocating / opportunity is going to work but you support your Aries in their Aries-ness and with all the love you can muster...

And don't make it worse by adding, 'It will all end in tears.' It might, but it's likely to be your tears, not theirs. An Aries doesn't mind making mistakes. They do mind being prevented from making mistakes by other people concerned that they'll get hurt, go bust, get overdrawn, be ill, or even, God forbid, 'fail'.

I asked Elaine what she feels her support needs are:

'We still need reassurance and to feel safe and loved. Don't ever try to squelch any ambitions that are good. Don't ever say, "You can't do that" – unless it's illegal, of course.'

'What have we been getting all wrong?' I asked her.

'We Aries are searching for an identity of our own. We may appear arrogant at times, but that is because we are trying out new stuff and we want to be proud of going out there and trying on many different hats until we find the right fit for us. Let us learn for ourselves. Let us learn that sometimes we get burned, but that is part of the process. We do learn from our mistakes. Let us be who we are: explorers.'

Aries would *rather* fail than not give something their best shot.

I know a lovely Aries lady who wanted a baby. She'd suffered a number of miscarriages, had also had cancer, which she had recovered from, and her husband didn't mind if he did or didn't have more children. *She* wanted another child and he supported her...

So she got pregnant, and lost the baby. She got pregnant again, and lost that baby. She got pregnant a third time and got lucky and the baby lived full-term and grew up happy and healthy.

And then she 'tried' again.

Four more pregnancies resulted in early miscarriage. She went to see a holistic therapist about her health and refused to discuss with him the fact that she'd lost so many babies. *He* wanted to explore her determination, in the face of such bad odds, to 'try' for another baby. *She* wanted help with her headaches, so he got short shrift and she went to find another therapist.

Don't waste your time or theirs when an Aries has a project in hand. Leave them to find out, themselves, how things are, and in the long run everyone will be happy.

Chapter Seven

The Solutions

Keeping in mind what we've discussed so far about Aries, there really shouldn't be any need for you to read this chapter, but I've written it to push home the point that even though your Aries is an Aries, the other signs' influence in their chart will colour how they will relate to any help you might offer.

For example, someone with a lot of Cancer in their chart, even though they might be Aries Sun, will enjoy cuddles and soft touch and gentle care.

So here are some easy-to-use solutions for your Aries, if they've hit a hard patch in life and need some assistance.

Aries Asc or Moon

There is only one way to help here and that is to do something physical and/or sporty. Get on your running shoes or sports kit, and meet up with your Aries and get them to thrash their feelings out on the tennis court, basketball court, football pitch, or anywhere that moves the body. If you want them to feel better, don't bother with conversation; ACTION is the needed solution. Try and avoid anything that might put you at risk, so don't arrange a fencing session or boxing match – you might find you're the target for any stressful feelings!

Taurus Asc or Moon

The energies with the Aries/Taurus combination are aimed at wanting to feel safe and secure. Arrange a firm date and take your Aries/Taurus to a good slap-up meal, or at the very least cook for them. Slow down and match their body language. Get the chocolates and good wine out and ensure they're feeling relaxed. If you're any good at massage, you will be seen as their saviour, or hire someone qualified to smooth away those angsty energies with fragrant oils and soothing movements. The body needs to be attended to, so deep breathing and tactile contact is needed. The mind can be sorted out later.

Gemini Asc or Moon

Now you will have to have your wits about you and your ears peeled back. Pay attention to every word they say. An Aries/Gemini needs to feel heard and understood. If you repeat back a summary of what they've told you, you're on solid ground. Maybe even get them to write down how they feel, as they'll be so speeding around with questions and remarks and jibes and damning one-liners, you might get singed in the process. When they've written as much as they can, change the subject and do something totally different like going for a walk or meeting up with some other friends.

Cancer Asc or Moon

An Aries/Cancer combo will want to *feel* their emotions. They will be overcome with them, in fact, which might make them a little weepy. Get the tissues out and mirror their body language and, when they've cried their ocean, wrap them up in some soft, fluffy blanket and tuck them up on the sofa. Listen carefully to their words and look underneath what they're actually saying; tune into their feelings, which at this moment will be like a wave, overwhelming and wet. In a little while, the wave will recede and they'll be back to normal. Hugs! Did I mention hugs? They will be needed in abundance when Aries/Cancer gets to feeling down, so snuggle up and embrace the hurt away.

Leo Asc or Moon

Do NOT ignore a Aries/Leo. They want to feel acknowledged and included. They will be running around, sighing and being dramatic and shouting 'Off with their heads!' or similar drastic cries. Ignore the drama but don't ignore the person. You could ask, 'What will help you *NOW*?' and do whatever they suggest, provided it's legal and do-able. Agree that life is unfair and lay out the red-carpet of one-to-one special treatment with personal inclusion. Say their name more than once, in friendly tones. This always works a treat, and nod your head in agreement to their feelings, which by now will be buzzing around at an alarming rate. Get them to take one good, deep breath in…and slowly let it out, and their sunny self will soon return.

Virgo Asc or Moon

With the Aries/Virgo person you will need to ooze calm and centeredness. Remember the Flower Essence Centaury and administer 2 drops in water before you attempt any other form of help. What is needed is for their brains to switch off. Aries have active, fast-moving bodies; couple that with Virgo's need for precision and all they can think about is how to 'make things better', and they will be striving to 'do' millions of things about it all. Worst-case scenario will see them like rabbits in the headlamps, frozen to one recurring idea, which they find hard to break out of. Soothing music, Tai Chi, gentle body exercise, sensible food and lots of good sleep will bring them back to earth perfectly.

Libra Asc or Moon

Most Aries/Libra combos will be worried about relationships… or 'The One'. If they've fallen out with their nearest and dearest you will find a weepy, questioning person needing careful handling. First off, don't give them any choices. This is, after all, the person who will be deliberating a choice. Come or go? Stay or leave? Right or wrong? Help the process by *not* giving a choice, and sweep them away to somewhere beautiful and presentable where they can experience a better balance of ideas. Don't correct them or get into an argument, and don't talk too much; let the place you have chosen calm them enough to reconfigure and let them feel centred. Yoga, gentle massage, light, tuneful music – harp or something equally soothing – will work well too.

Scorpio Asc or Moon

Stand back! Don't get too close when Aries/Scorpio lets rip. You will find them consumed with the passion of deep, excruciating, painful feelings, and revenge might be on the agenda. Be aware that they will want to resolve whatever is going on with drastic, painful solutions. If you think about the colour of deep red blood, you will get an idea of how they're feeling. It sucks! It's horrible! They want an END to it all (whatever is happening to them).

Get them to write the person or problem a letter. Tell them to put ALL their feelings into the writing...then make a bonfire or light a candle and safely watch the pain and anguish be consumed by the flames. Be firm. Be 'there'. You can't do much other than wait out the feelings, which, like all feelings, will eventually subside.

Sagittarius Asc or Moon

To get an Aries/Sag to admit that there is a problem will be difficult. It's generally 'them' that are the problem, so 'they' will have to be the focus of the solution. Get some aged texts. The Bible, or other friendly spiritual writings by a favourite guru or lama or other spiritual leader, and either lend or buy the book for them. Arrange a trip away to some far-off exotic land where they can 'escape' from the everyday-ness that has caused the problem. If finances are tight, get them to a local foreign restaurant or a talk where the focus is on far-off and distant lands. McDonald's or take-aways won't work the same. They need to be surrounded by people and conversations that are *different* from their own, so they can feel free to have the thoughts/feelings and opinions they're having. If they enjoy sport, go to a game – anything that will be different from where they are at the moment. Change, exotic change, is paramount.

Capricorn Asc or Moon

As Capricorn is ruled by Saturn and loves serious, sensible solutions, an Aries/Cappie will want advice and guidance from someone older and hopefully wiser than them. Their main worry will be about 'the future' and they will be concerned that they've ruined their chances, or missed an opportunity. If you can find someone who has 'been there and done that', they will start to thaw a little. You could of course go one better and help them discover their ancestral line and help them research their family tree, as Aries/Cap loves that which is ancient and tried and tested. A short visit to a stately home or traditional concert might also help...and do NOT rush them to recover. They need time and space.

Aquarius Asc or Moon

If you can imagine the weirdest and wackiest solution to their problem, you will have found the elixir of happiness. Aries/Aquarius loves that which can only be defined as 'unusual'. Stay away from mainstream ideas; go for that which is different and unregulated and you'll have the happiest Aries/Aqua on the planet. Staying up late discussing Life, the Universe and Everything will also go down well. You could take them out for a short trip to see street-entertainers, or meet with some art students or people co-creating an ecological event. You could plug them into a simulator so they can experience some wacky occurrence, or play a computer game that doesn't have any set rules. Anything that is not normal, not regular, not Earth-based. They want to feel connected to some life-changing human consciousness.

Pisces Asc or Moon

Get out your Angel cards, light the incense or some candles. Put on soft music, get away from 'life' and 'humans', and touch into the outer reaches of all that is cosmic and divine. Any form of divination will be welcomed. They will be worrying about their next life, and their karma, so reassure them you've got that covered. The spiritual solution must be credible and not *too* fantastic. Keep their feet on the ground but let their mind go where nothing hurts and no one can intervene. Meditation, hypnotherapy, relaxation, angels, fairies, stone circles or making a pilgrimage – all will be welcome, and at the very least a long, fragrant bath with a big 'Do Not Disturb' sign on the door!

Chapter Eight

Appreciating Tactics

Now that you've learned a little about Aries the Sun sign, we're now going to go through the different ways an Aries will manifest in your life. You could have an Aries boyfriend, boss or relative, and need to know how that positive, searching energy will make itself known in your life.

Your Aries Child

The thing about kids is that they express emotion. They don't hold back. If they want to cry, they cry, and if they are in a good mood, they're in a good mood.
Eddie Murphy

The quote above is from Eddie Murphy, who is an Aries, and was a child once, as we all were. I think he sums up perfectly what it's like being an Aries child.

They have emotions.

They don't have, and may never have, a self-awareness mechanism. They will shout and scream and have tantrums, unless you acknowledge exactly how they're feeling NOW. Not tomorrow, not what they did or said yesterday (that's far too long ago)…No, you have to 'be' there when they're telling you how they feel.

Really 'be'.

Now this is easy enough when your little bundle of joy is a babe-in-arms. We expect babes to be like this, but when your babe is a little bigger and going to school, they're going to have to learn to share ('Share! What's that?!'), because if they don't, they'll get tormented by the other kids, or pulled up by the teachers, or excluded – you get the picture.

Teach your Aries child, from a very early age, that you love them as they are. They don't need to change to have your love. They don't need to 'win' it or 'fight' for it; your love just exists like the wind and the rain and the Sun.

Teach your little Aries bundle, too, that everyone is not the same as them. That other people have ideas and thoughts and views on stuff that might be completely different from theirs and IT DOESN'T MATTER. What matters is what they do, not what they think.

Your Aries child will be the first one in school to stand up to bullies or teachers that are harsh. I expect when Oliver Twist asked, 'Please sir, can I have some more?' that was an Aries voice speaking, as he wasn't scared by Mr Bumble and was motivated by wanting to help his fellow orphans.

Poppy describes the more familiar side of an Aries child when I asked her, 'What would an Aries child need when growing up?'

> *'Well, I would say you would have to have a lot of patience and understanding, because growing up I can remember being very stroppy, bossy (I was nicknamed "Bossy Boots") and stubborn – any shouting or telling-off made me even more stubborn. If I was "coaxed" or "fussed over", it was a different story.'*

Mandy is a retired teacher and lives in Chicago, USA:

> *'As a child I had quite a temper, which my mom worked hard to teach me to tame. Tame our tempers, give us responsibilities/challenges, put us in charge of something. Trust us.'*

She also tells us:

> *'Linda Goodman says it well in her book Love Signs (pp. 70–72): "Very few people are aware of how frantically Aries men and women*

(and children) seek acceptance...The Rams are not always as tough as they act...Aries people don't mean to step on anyone's sensitive feelings, (but) they can be inconsiderate and thoughtless without realizing it...The typical Ram would never hurt anyone on purpose...Aries people have little or no awareness of this particular weakness in themselves (sensitivity to hurt) – it clashes with their self image of strength."'

And as Linda Goodman also wisely advises in her *Sun Signs*:

'Parents and teachers should never forget that Aries children glow under praise and doggedly proceed to top their own efforts, but they sputter like fire-crackers under attack and lose all incentive to try.'

So praise your Aries child's achievements, ignore their failures, and if you really want to spur them on, tell them what they've done is good and you love them just as they are, but maybe it's because they're not as bright or clever as Jill or Jack...and your Aries child will now have someone to compare to and compete with and will rise to the challenge.

Here is Karen, whom we met earlier, and who has an Aries father. She tells us a little about being an Aries child:

'Since being a parent I have to say to a certain extent I am my father's daughter. I can be critical. It doesn't come naturally to me to praise my children. I have to remind myself to do it because I'm very aware of low self-esteem and would not want them to have low self-esteem. So far, they are the complete opposite to me as a child and if anything they have way too much confidence – if that's possible – but still I feel proud and I must be doing something right! :) So what I'm saying is: don't be critical to an Aries child, because as you know we can take everything to heart and it can affect our future.'

Elaine discusses an Aries child's needs:

'Love and kindness. Take an interest in what they are interested in at the time. Encourage some form of art. Set time aside to ask if they have any worries they want to talk about. Plenty of space, emotionally. Outdoor activities. Social time with peers. Explain why there are things that are just the way they are, and share empathy. Lots of hugs and kisses. No practical jokes. Don't laugh at them. Encouragement with education. Tell them often that they are loved. Say "I love you" out loud often. Hugs. Let them have their feelings and thoughts without trying to change them through scolding. Compliment them on how clever they are, even if you don't understand how they can be so smart."'

Your Aries Boss

I know a number of Aries bosses. Male and Female. One in particular comes to mind. Our family employed him to supervise a care package for my youngest sister, and I made an appointment to meet him.

He arrived on time, well dressed but not overly formal. I explained what we needed and he got out his calculator, made some quick calculations, summarized exactly what I needed, and assured me there was nothing to worry about and this was 'do-able'.

He employed a team of devoted carers, trained them exactly in what was needed, and all went well. After a number of months, my sister's health took a dramatic turn for the worse and care was needed round the clock. I still don't know how he managed to keep his team working long hours, at two different locations, with nurses and doctors all telling his team what to do. No one fell out with anyone. They all pulled together, and somehow or other Mr Aries kept the rosters up to date, the staff paid and everyone still working together.

Nothing fazed him.

Not even when staff went sick, or got pregnant, or left on the spot or got snowed in. We had various 'incidents' and 'safeguarding meetings' with the council (local government), clashes with other care teams who were also helping, and behind the scenes he'd answer his phone immediately or send daily text messages keeping everyone working to keep my sister cared for and well.

He even spent three days in hospital himself with pneumonia and just wouldn't accept that he might need to slow down. That just spurred him on all the more to get everything back on an even keel. I couldn't rate him more highly. He took on a job that your average manager a) wouldn't understand and b) would have dropped like a hot coal when the going got tough. This got tough and he went into overdrive to keep everything together.

Needless to say, I thanked him as and when it was needed. Pointed out when things needed tweaking. I hope he felt appreciated. He certainly *was* appreciated by me and the carers and our family. So much so, when we had to lay the team off because my sister went into a residential nursing care-home, one of the carers was heartbroken as she'd never been as involved all down the line as she had with this manager.

He treated them all exactly as he would like to be treated himself, as professional, talented people.

Here is Sandy telling us about a business lady she knows:

'A former colleague of mine is an Aries gal and she is quite simply the most incredible businesswoman. She could sell hot sauce to a chilli pepper – she is absolutely dazzling. Stellar career in public relations and now she sells her own jewellery line on HSN. I have always had immense admiration for her, and her Aries energy is honestly irresistible.'

Your (Female) Aries Lover
The best way to learn about dating a certain Sun sign is to read

what they write on the dating websites. Most people are good at writing about themselves, so it gives us a little insight into their likes and dislikes.

Here is a young lady called Charlotte who is looking for love:

'This kind of feels like writing my CV and I have to resist putting "I am a hard-working individual with excellent attention to detail and good communication and interpersonal skills."

'I love spending time with friends and family, eating out, watching films, going for walks and making the most of being in London. I enjoy travelling the world and there are a lot more places I would like to visit. I like to run on Hampstead Heath, weather permitting. Love getting away for long weekends in the country, or abroad to sunnier climes.

'One of my hobbies is photography so I often have my camera with me, always taking lots of photos. Some turn out great, others not so much. Enjoy going to art galleries and exhibitions, getting inspiration from them.

'I like to eat out and try new restaurants and have spent some of the summer trying the top restaurants and bars around London. I like going to gigs – have already seen the Boss this summer...He is my hero!

'I like to be challenged and experience new exciting adventures.'

Who I'm Looking For:
'I would like to meet someone who is fun and enjoys doing new things, someone who doesn't take themselves too seriously and can make me laugh.'

Unlike any other sign of the Zodiac, it doesn't matter what sign you are, if an Aries fancies you. I can't tell you the amount of people I know who are dating an Aries and their Sun signs don't really match too well. If you're a Water sign, you might find your Aries lover a little too fast, but they themselves won't care one jot about that. If they love you, they love you.

That's that.

So, to date an Aries lady successfully, just be yourself. Don't pretend to be anything other than who you are. If you're penniless and living in a shack, it won't matter to her. If you're a millionaire, it also won't make any difference. You can't bribe or buy her love. Just be who you are and she will love you, warts and all.

And if she tells you she loves you, accept that fact graciously because she will be telling you her truth. An Aries lady is very unlikely to love someone for anything other than liking your company.

However, what you mustn't do is pour cold water on her ideas/hobbies/views. Just keep your opinions to yourself. Don't tell her to lose weight, or dress differently, or be more or less of who she is, or you'll only see dust where she was standing.

If you show a positive approach to life, can enjoy the simple pleasures that life brings, and accept her for all of who she is, you'll have her love for ever and ever.

Your (Male) Aries Lover

Here is some valid advice from Louise, who knows a thing or two about Aries men:

> 'A girlfriend of mine that was involved with an Aries for more than 40 years claims that a heated debate can be much like foreplay to them. Like one of those scenes in the old-fashioned black and white movies where the woman's telling this guy what she really thinks of him, she's really letting him have it – and then he suddenly and unexpectedly grabs her and lays a long, passionate kiss on her.'

Aquarius author Lara has dated two Aries men:

> 'I met the first one at a party and we flirted outrageously. He

wanted to get together with me very quickly and kept turning up at my house. He was very persistent but I wanted to find out more about him. I thought he was very attractive and charming. He was friends with some friends of mine and they said he was a lovely guy. We eventually went out for about a year and a half. He was indeed lovely and generous. He would do anything for his friends. However, his life was in constant turmoil. He refused to have any sort of permanence in his life. He lived in three different places all the time I knew him. He worked as a lorry driver but he said he only did it for the money. He didn't like to have any sort of "label". He was infuriating, as he hated any sort of schedules or arrangements. He just wanted to see me whenever he wanted. He would also disappear for weeks on end. Although he was fun to be with, he had a chip on his shoulder about the fact that he didn't have as much as all his friends. He didn't have a house or proper job etc....In the end he dumped me suddenly and he couldn't really explain why. There may have been another woman involved. Women found him very attractive, not just because he was good-looking but because he was emotional and spontaneous.'

In the second relationship, she tells us:

'He also wanted to get together with me very quickly. He asked me to live with him after we had been going out for six months. I said "No", it was too early. He said he was pleased he had "at last" found a woman who was "intelligent and independent" as all his other women had been "dependent" on him. He liked it that I had a job and was an author. His previous love life was complicated. He seemed to have chosen stormy women. He had two ex-wives and a son with his last girlfriend and two other sons with other women. He was in a constant battle with the mother of his youngest son over access issues...

'At first our relationship was feisty and we did plenty of "different" things together. However, that eventually changed.

'He also hating planning anything and it was a real effort to get him to go away at weekends or do anything different on a Saturday other than go down the supermarket or watch rugby or go and see his mum. Despite all this, when we did get on, we got on well. We had our best conversations when we were in the car!!! He drove like a maniac.

'He didn't really like it that I was his intellectual equal and that I earned just as much money as him, possibly more. I think he wanted to be a hero and be looked up to. He wanted more status than he had, but he hated his job and his boss bullied him. He thought of himself as an action man, but he didn't go anywhere or do very much. He had a motorbike in the garden that he never got fixed and he never got rid of. It just sat there going rusty. He was passionate about Tai Chi and his health, but he smoked like a chimney.

'He was full of contradictions.

'He ended our relationship very suddenly. It was after he had been depressed when he left his job. I basically supported him during this time. He got a new job and new confidence and that was it – I was history. He admitted that he felt "in my shadow" as I was reasonably well known as an author. He also admitted he was scared of getting "old and boring" like his parents. He said he wanted a partner who "cared for him" more than I did and that he had felt abandoned when I went off on writing tours. So much for wanting an intelligent and independent woman!!! Sigh.'

The following gentleman, called Sam, gives us some ideas about who he is, and what he needs in a relationship:

'I think I lead an interesting life – I love music, play bass guitar in a band, and try to see live music when I can. I play tennis and go to the gym fairly regularly.

'I'm in the fourth year of an English degree course with the Open University – oh, and I started my own business a few years ago, which takes up a lot of my time...Ermmm, does it sound like

I'm really busy? :-) I would hope that I could find time for someone new in my life, especially if they were witty, intelligent, attractive and sincere...Any offers?

'I do have a wicked, rather sarcastic sense of humour, which past girlfriends have said I use as something of a defence mechanism. I am quite a moral person and I really appreciate integrity. I'm worried that I'm getting a little serious as I get older – is that a bad thing?'

Some Things I Like:

- *Avaaz – a great website – launched in 2007 with a simple democratic mission: organise citizens of all nations to close the gap between the world we have and the world most people everywhere want. Have a look.*
- *Seinfeld*
- *Books – I think I'm addicted to bookshops!*
- *The Smiths*
- *Going to the theatre, especially to see Shakespeare at Stratford!*
- *Playing guitar*
- *Chatting about world affairs, religion, politics, and idiotic conversations that go nowhere but for some reason are really entertaining*
- *The White Lies – saw them recently in Bristol and I have to say they were brilliant!*
- *Have I Got News for You*
- *Travelling – though I don't think I'll be doing any for a while :o(*
- *Lists – but then I am a man so I think I'm excused, ha ha*
- *Ermmm...I'll add more things as I think of them...*

Who I'm Looking For:

'Obviously physical attraction and chemistry is important – I'm drawn to people with wit, intelligence, integrity, and an interest in the world.'

Notice how one of his likes was the charity website that 'unites people from around the world to work for the common good'. This is a very Aries undertaking. They will always stand up for the underdog.

Notice also how his 'Who I'm Looking For' is less than two sentences. It doesn't really matter what you're like as long as you let him be the way he is, and have a mutual attraction – and he will know immediately if he has it or not.

Girls! Don't waste your love on an Aries man that doesn't fancy you. If that initial spark just isn't there, there is no way he will be able to create it later.

Don't 'wait' for him to fall in love. If he hasn't done it in seconds flat in meeting you, it's never going to happen. I sometime think that speed dating must have been 'invented' by an Aries. Try it if you are an Aries; you might hit lucky!

What to Do If Your Aries Relationship Ends

Fire sign

If you are a Fire sign – our friend Aries, Leo or Sagittarius – you will need something active and exciting to help you get over your relationship ending.

You will also need to use the element of Fire in your healing process.

Get a nice night-light candle, light it and recite: 'I ... (your name) do let you ... (your ex-Aries' name) go, in freedom and with love, so that I am free to attract my true soul-love.'

Leave the night light in a safe place to completely burn away. Allow at least an hour. In the meantime gather up any belongings or possessions that are your now ex-lover's and deliver them back to your Aries. It's polite to telephone first and notify your ex when you will be arriving.

If you have any photos of you together or other mementos or even gifts, don't be in a rush to destroy them, as some Fire signs are prone to do. Better to put them away in a box in the attic or garage until you feel a little less upset.

In a few months' time, go through the box and keep the things you like and give away the things you don't.

Earth sign

If you are an Earth sign – Taurus, Virgo or Capricorn – you will feel less inclined to do something dramatic or outrageous. It might also take you slightly longer to recover your equilibrium, so allow yourself a few weeks and a maximum of three months to grieve.

You will be using the Earth element to help your healing, with the use of some trusty crystals.

The best crystals to use are the ones associated with your Sun sign and also with protection:

Taurus = Emerald
Virgo = Agate
Capricorn = Onyx

Cleanse your crystal in fresh running water. Wrap it in some pretty silk fabric, then go on a walk into the countryside. When you find a suitable spot that is quiet and where you won't be disturbed, dig a small hole and place your crystal in the ground.

Spend a few minutes thinking about your relationship, the good times and the bad. Forgive yourself for any mistakes you may have made.

Imagine a beautiful plant growing from the ground where you have buried your crystal, and the plant blossoming and growing strong.

This will represent your new love that will be with you when the time is right.

Air sign

If you're an Air sign – Gemini, Libra or Aquarius – you might want to talk about what happened first, before you finish the relationship. Air signs need reasons and answers, and can waste precious life-energy looking for those answers. You might need to meet with your Aries to tell him/her exactly what you think/thought about his/her opinions, ideas and thoughts. You might also be tempted to tell him/her what you think about them now, which I do *not* recommend.

Far better to put those thoughts into a tangible form by writing your ex-Aries a letter.

This is not a letter that you are actually going to post, but you are going to put into it as much energy *as if* you were actually going to send it.

Write to them thus: 'Dear Aries, I expect you will be happy now in your new life, but there are a few things I would like to know and understand before I say goodbye.'

Then list all the annoying, aggravating, upsetting ideas that your (now ex) Aries indulged in. Make a list as long as you like. Put in as much detail as you feel comfortable with, including things like how many times they didn't respect your views, or were grumpy with your best friends, or didn't return your calls.

Keep writing till you can write no more, then end your letter with something like: 'Even though we were not suited, and I suffered because of this, I wish you well on your path.' Or some other positive comment.

Then tear your letter into teeny little pieces and put them into a small container. We are now going to use the element of Air to rectify the situation.

Take a trip to somewhere windy and high, like the top of a hill, and when you're ready, open your container and sprinkle a few random pieces of your letter into the wind. Don't use the entire letter or you run the risk of littering, just enough pieces to be significant.

Watch those little pieces of paper fly into the distance and imagine them connecting with the nature spirits.

Your relationship has now ended.

Water sign

If you are a Water sign – Cancer, Scorpio or Pisces – you might find it more difficult to recover quickly from your relationship. You might find yourself weeping at inopportune moments, or when you hear 'your' song on the radio, or when you see other couples happily being in each other's company. You might lie awake at night worrying that you have ruined your life, and your ex-Aries is having all the fun. As you might have gathered by now, this is unlikely. Your ex might be as upset as you.

Your emotional healing therefore needs to incorporate the Water element.

As you are capable of weeping for England, the next time you are in floods of tears capture one small teardrop and place it into a small glass. Have one handy just for this purpose. Decorate it if you feel like it. Small flowers, stars, or twinkly things.

Now fill your glass to the top with tap water and place it on a table.

Then recite the following:

'This loving relationship with you … (your ex-Aries' name) has ended.
I reach out across time and space to you.
My tears will wash away the hurt I feel.
I release you from my heart, mind and soul.
We part in peace.'

And then slowly drink the water. Imagine your hurt dissolving away, freeing you from all anxieties and releasing you from sadness.

Then spend the next few weeks being nice to yourself. If you need to talk, find someone you trust, and confide in them. Keep tissues handy.

Your Aries Friend

I have had a number of Aries friends over the years but, as I am a Water sign, eventually they sped off into the distance. One friend has stayed in my life for a jolly long time and I think that's because of various planetary compatibilities and also because we don't see each other too much. I'm not exhausted by her speediness and she's not deflated by my wateriness.

Alexandra is a Gemini and she tells us about her Aries friend:

'There are only two things that come to mind from all my Aries experience.

'First – they are stubborn as hell. It's impossible to argue with them; if they get something into their heads, they will never change their mind. But you can reach the point where you agree to disagree and they do respect another person for having a firm opinion too.

'Second – they are great friends, very reliable. And usually they're the kind you can call in the middle of the night and they will come over, no matter how far they are, if you really need them.'

I'm not so sure about the first observation; I suppose it depends what you define as stubborn. I don't bother trying to change people's minds about things. Acceptance is much easier.

However, I definitely agree with Alexandra's second comment. From my experience, if there was a world war or my house got bombed or my car stolen, or I was mugged, I would certainly want my Aries friend to be there to help me. In a crisis an Aries is brilliant. They can work out in seconds what's important and what isn't. They won't mess around and will get straight to either a solution or at the very least 'next steps'.

If anything dramatic happened, I'd want an Aries to be there first on the scene.

To get on best with your Aries, this ability to assist in a crisis is definitely a two-way street. If you don't respond as swiftly as *them* when *they* hit a hard patch, they won't complain – you'll just be off their Xmas card list and you are unlikely to see them ever again.

Your Aries Mother

I know a number of Aries mothers. All shapes and sizes. And because of the work I do, I meet a lot in my private practice. I once did an analysis of the signs of my clients, and surprisingly enough, that year Aries topped the list of people that needed my help. Now, with Aries being such a self-sufficient sign, you might question why Aries is high on the list of people needing my help. I'll tell you why.

Aries love 'an expert'. If you're an expert at something, an Aries will consult you. You have to be 'the' expert in whatever you do though. If an Aries can't work something out, or they need a diagnosis or advice or something they're not qualified to do, they will go to whoever is the most experienced in that field.

Obviously, in my line of work, my experience is 'understanding the future' and, since Aries is a Cardinal sign and rather future-orientated, being able to work in that field makes me more knowledgeable than them. (Unless of course...they are an astrologer themselves.)

Aries mothers will consult me if they can't imagine or work out how something might turn out, or if they've been struggling with some negative situation for a while. They take their role seriously and work hard to 'be' the perfect mother. As we know, being perfect and motherhood don't go hand in hand, so give your Aries mother some slack if she's working really hard at being all things to everyone.

'I'm an Aries mother and I tell my daughter I love her every day and give her loads of hugs and kisses. I don't, however, give in to my

daughter when she cries – unless she has hurt herself. This is because I don't want my daughter falling into bad habits and using manipulation to get what she wants (she's a Scorpio, so she may well end up like that if I don't train her) and I want her to grow up to be a strong woman, so I try not to molly-coddle her. I feel it's important to show your child you love them, but you also have to be strict and teach them to have control.'

Gemini Sandy talks about her mother, who not only has her Sun in Aries, but also her Mars, making her more inclined to deal with things in an active manner:

'My mother has this placement. She really has outbursts sometimes.'

I found this interesting website called Aries Mommy:

'Welcome to Aries Mommy! Pour yourself a drink, pull up a chair and stay awhile. Do you like to cook, craft, read, or work out? Or maybe you just like to know that you aren't the only woman who wonders if she will ever have a spotless house, well-behaved kids, and a killer manicure (all at the same time).

'I am a proud United States Marine Corps wife, a mother to four sweet children, and a woman who has decided it is time to stop filtering her opinions. It turns out that life is a lot more fun when the filter is off! Who knew that my brain was filtering out all the interesting things! If you like to have someone tell you like it is and remove all the fluff, then you are at the right place.

'Sexy Sergeant and I have been married for nearly 11 years and together for nearly 15. Over the years we have had our share of life lessons. The Marines currently have us living in New York. Our four children take up most of my time and energy. The poor kids are learning to cook, clean, and be responsible for themselves. Not to mention how embarrassed they become when we show them that

even as adults, having fun is mandatory. As a family, we enjoy visiting new places, trying new foods, and discussing the things around us. When I am not cooking or cleaning, I enjoy reading and working out. Though not at the same time; I am not coordinated enough to read a novel and walk on the treadmill. During the summer of 2011, I was a 'Mamavation Mom'. That journey helped to push me into a health and fitness mindset, as well as to remind me to take care of myself. Now the passion for fitness and healthier cooking is featured here.'

I loved the way she was married to a marine, had organised a 'mama-vation' event to motivate other mothers to be fit and healthy, and the words: 'If you like to have someone tell you like it is...' which are typically Aries.

Not everyone enjoys having an Aries mother. Here is Chantelle, a Capricorn young lady:

'My Aries mom is driving me crazy. Why is she so rude and self-centered?

'Oh and by the way I'm a Capricorn. I have been feeling awfully depressed lately. I've been laid off, diagnosed with a virus, and lost my two last friends because they used me. All I really have left is my boyfriend and his buddies which I'm very grateful for. Sometimes I get angry with my mom because she doesn't comfort me. Sometimes I'll say nothing because I'm not ready to talk to her about anything. But while I still mope around, she takes it that I have an attitude and then there she goes! She gossips to my sister (Gemini), and even my niece (Cancer) who is 9! How I always have an attitude and blah blah...

'I have opened up to my mom so many times about how I feel and sometimes she mistakes my sadness for being mad and it hurts even more. I'm just so tired of trying to get her to understand me. It's just so hard because my sister and my mom seem to easily get along. They're like best friends. I feel like none of them really understand

me. So while I'm depressed, I get her yelling at me and making things worse. I swear I will hang myself; this woman drives me crazy. :('

This question was posted on a website, and very quickly (!) an Aries mother replied with some suggestions:

'Aries woman here – First of all get your mom an Astrology book and MAKE her read about herself! More importantly – MAKE her read about you!

'Reading about Astrology saved my life. I used to think I was crazy until I understood myself!

'There can be no good relationship without understanding that we are all different people and we should all be accepted for EXACTLY who we are!

'It seems to me like you need to work on the accepting part. You want her to accept you for who you are, but are you willing to do the same to her?

'JUST KNOW THAT YOU ARE VERY DIFFERENT PEOPLE, SO NEVER STOP BEING YOURSELF NO MATTER WHAT ANYONE SAYS!

'I understand she is your mom, but she is still human, you know. She may have had a lousy mom too, you never know. I have parents like that, and I always felt like I had to make the effort to be close to them – heck, I still do, ha ha. They are Pisces and Cancer. TOTALLY DIFFERENT than me, an Aries.

'What can I say? Relationships take a lot of work from both parties involved, and the sooner you learn this, the better!

'I would try talking to your mom and having an HONEST HEARTFELT TALK AND LET HER KNOW HOW SHE MAKES YOU FEEL. I'M SURE SHE WILL STOP IMMEDIATELY. SHE PROBABLY DOESN'T KNOW HOW MUCH SHE IS HURTING YOU!'

As you can see in the above answer, the Aries mom knows that she can't change anyone, that she is who she is, and for Chantelle to get on better with her Aries mom, she will have to agree...to disagree, and be honest with the way she is feeling.

It's also no good if you've got an Aries mom to drop subtle hints. They won't work.

Or to bend the truth about how you feel. If you feel bad, say so!

Of all the signs of the Zodiac more likely to be defensive of their children, Aries mother is that sign.

Linda Goodman, the author of the best-selling *Sun Signs* and later *Linda Goodman's Love Signs*, was an Aries with Moon in Scorpio. Her daughter Sarah was an award-winning actress that sadly died in suspicious circumstances in December 1973. Linda never came to terms with her daughter's death and by February 1980 had offered a $50,000 reward for information 'on the whereabouts' of Sarah.[11]

Linda was convinced that Sarah was a victim of mistaken identity and homicide. The case was never resolved and Linda died never knowing what had truly happened to her daughter.

She wrote about her feelings in a short piece of fiction in her *Love Signs*:[12]

Let us look again at Sally's mother, a very sad-eyed woman. Now that we look at her more closely and remember the gaiety of the old days, all gone now, just because she had lost her babe...Look at her in her chair, where she has fallen asleep. The corner of her mouth, where one looks first, the corner Sally always kissed, is almost withered up.

An Aries mother will fight to her last, living breath to protect her children. Even if she might complain about them occasionally, or be a little sharp, or pull them up if they misbehave, underneath is someone who will protect them and save them from any outside harm.

I have a dear Gemini friend whose mum was Aries. She was strong and determined. My friend has a Libra Ascendant and she could never understand why her mum was so direct and forceful. It caused her an enormous amount of grief.

It was only when her mother died that she realised how much she had been a supporter of her father, because when her mother died, her father went to pieces. Mother had done *everything* for Father and now he couldn't manage the loneliness or lack of support from his Aries stalwart.

Here we have a Capricorn young man called Mario, talking about his Aries mother. His parents got divorced when he was small. His father is a Pisces:

'It's interesting. She always wanted to take care of everything, and she would manage that if we had more luck. She had three houses to manage and her job. I'm really surprised how well she managed that. Or how well she managed to hide all the things that bothered her. She still feels and looks younger than she really is. More capable than many that I've met in my life. She was always realistic; she gave up many of her dreams to provide for everyone. I really admire her.'

Your Aries mother will work hard to manage not only her mothering, but also her career and other elderly members of the family.

Your Aries Father

Over the years I have met a number of Aries fathers in my private practice. They don't admit to enjoying being a parent, but secretly they love what having a child brings.

It's not always an easy journey.

Presidential candidate Al Gore and his wife Tipper were crossing the street in Baltimore, in April 1989, when their six-year-old son Albert suddenly bolted from his father's hand and was hit by a car.

Their youngest child flew 30 ft. and slid along the pavement 20 more.

'I ran to his side and held him and called his name, but he was motionless, limp and still, without breath or pulse,' his father wrote. 'His eyes were open with the nothingness stare of death, and we prayed, the two of us, there in the gutter, with only my voice.' Two nurses happened upon the scene and treated the boy until an ambulance arrived. For the next month, Al and Tipper stayed by his side at [the hospital]. For many months after, Gore wrote, 'our lives were consumed with the struggle to restore his body and spirit...The catharsis I went through beginning on April 3, 1989, was a time when those lessons really hit home for me, because I was suddenly open to them.'

He had become a different kind of husband, a different kind of father – and, he insists, a different kind of politician. When Al is asked how, he says, 'Where don't you see it? It's pervasive.'[13]

It took the near-death experience of his youngest son for this Aries father to realise how short life is, and how precious the lives of his children are.

We met Karen, the massage therapist and single mother to two young daughters, earlier. She's an Aries, with an Aries father. She tells us about their difficult relationship:

'My dad was very critical, bossy and quite negative (my dad is an Aries). Him being critical did nothing for my self-esteem at all. I was always that kid who would sit at the back of the class. Never put my hand up even if I knew the answer – I'd still doubt myself. I was quite scared of my dad and terribly clumsy around him. I was so *nervous about making mistakes around him I'd actually then make mistakes, and he'd refer to himself as an ogre but saying he wasn't actually this! He was also very strict. Certain foods only on certain days, and I was allowed on a Sunday an apple cream turnover or 4 squares of chocolate!*

'I remember my beautiful step mum told me my dad was very proud of me, and I have to say I was shocked. I'd gone 27 years thinking I was a disappointment! I'm not sure what's more sad, me thinking that or the fact that he will never tell me himself. I make sure I tell my children every day I love them – oh, and think nothing of eating cake and lots of it on a Sunday morning. :)'

Stephanie has an Aries father too:

'My dad came to visit me in London last week – first time since I moved – and he was really lovely, warm and affectionate (a total Aries-in-a-good-mood) – must have been a good Aries-getting-on-with-Aries day.

'I've written about some of the trials and tribulations that I had when growing up, but I think we have worked through those issues and he also doesn't have the money worries he previously had. He is a real charmer and it's clear to see why he used to get away with murder – this sort of positive cheerfulness and total self-confidence that made him (just about) able to juggle 5 (I kid you not) girlfriends at the age of 18. I told him someone I knew had said he was good fun, and he reciprocated with, "Well, they're right. I am."'

To get on best with your Aries father, make his chart and find out what his Moon sign is and keep a note of when the Moon changes sign. That's on the astro.com website.

Be honest with him.

If you find his attitude towards you objectionable, tell him so, but don't expect him to understand right away. Don't be afraid of him either. That will just make things worse. If you have to stand up to him, do it – only once – and he won't cause you any fuss again.

Your Aries Sibling

Getting along with a sibling is always astrologically dependent on your elements and signs. If you are a Water or Earth sign, you relationship might be a bit more tricky. Hopefully your Moons will be in sync. Check your respective charts to get some clarity.

The following young lady doesn't know why she feels closer to her Aries sister than her Cancer sister. We know – because their mutual Fire-sign Suns are compatible:

'I'm a Leo Sun, Moon Aries with Virgo Ascendant. Why am I closer to my Aries sister than my Cancer sister?

'I could tell my Aries sister anything that I would never tell anyone, and I always feel comfortable being around her. Though she isn't as emotional, she can be very caring and supportive towards me every time I'm feeling down. I go downstairs to her room to visit her at least 4–5 times a week.

'But the Cancer sister...eh, I rarely ever talk to her. I never visit her, I never go to her for support, and I never felt close to her like I do with my Aries sister. And I don't know why!'

As we discussed earlier, Fire is a fast energy and Water is slow, so the Cancer and Leo sisters would be operating at very different speeds. Two Fire signs together make a speedy combination, one of mutual respect and joint excitement. Fire signs, more than any other signs, enjoy excitement and will fade and ebb if things aren't active and assertive.

To get along best with your Aries sibling, make sure you agree on certain things like who does what and when. Be clear about your feelings and don't be shy to tell them when you don't agree with something they're doing.

If you're Water or Earth, don't spend too much time together and make sure you have separate bedrooms or, at the very least, separate *parts* of the bedroom.

Be honest. That always works the best.

* * *

I hope you have enjoyed learning a little about the first sign of the Zodiac as much as I have enjoyed writing it. I hope also that you find the answers you are searching for. I am writing this while the Moon is in Aries in my home office in Bath and I am sending you peaceful thoughts and energies.

If we all understood each other a little better, maybe the world would be a more peaceful place to be.

Astrological Chart Information and Birth Data

(from astro-databank at www.astro.com
and www.astrotheme.com)

No accurate birth data

David Blaine, 4th April 1973, Brooklyn, NY, USA, Sun Aries, Moon either Aries or Taurus

Elton John, 25th March 1947, Pinner, England, UK, Sun Aries, Moon Taurus

Kofi Annan, 8th April 1938, Kumasi, Ghana, Sun Aries, Moon Cancer or Leo

Iris Chang, 28th March 1968, Princeton, NJ, USA, Sun Aries, Moon Aries

Isambard Kingdom Brunel, 8th April 1806, Portsmouth, England, UK, 12.55am, poss Sagittarius Ascendant, Sun in 4th, Moon Sagittarius

Johannes Sebastian Bach, 31st March 1685, Eisenach, Germany, Sun Aries, Moon Aquarius

Emma Thompson, 15th April 1959, London, England, UK, no birth time, Aries Sun, Cancer Moon

Abraham Maslow, 1st April 1908, Brooklyn, NY, USA, Aries Sun, Aries Moon

Ascendant

Samantha Fox, 15th April 1966, London, England, UK, 6am, Aries Ascendant, Sun in 1st, Moon Aquarius

Ali MacGraw, 1st April 1939, New York, NY, USA, 7.25am, Taurus Ascendant, Sun in 11th, Moon Virgo

Dirk Bogarde, 28th March 1921, Twickenham, England, UK, 8.30am, Gemini Ascendant, Sun in 10th, Moon Sagittarius

Emmylou Harris, 2nd April 1947, Birmingham, Alabama, USA, 12.10pm, Cancer Ascendant, Sun in 9th, Moon Virgo

Marvin Gaye, 2nd April 1939, Washington DC, USA, 11.59am, Cancer Ascendant, Sun in 9th, Moon Virgo

Celine Dion, 30th March 1968, Charlemagne, Quebec, Canada, 12.15pm, Leo Ascendant, Sun in 9th, Moon Aries

Warren Beatty, 30th March 1937, Richmond, VA, USA, 5.30pm, Virgo Ascendant, Sun in 7th, Moon Scorpio

Dudley Moore, 19th April 1935, Dagenham, England, UK, Libra Ascendant, Sun in 7th, Moon Scorpio

Charles Chaplin, 16th April 1889, London, England, UK, 8pm, Scorpio Ascendant, Sun in 6th, Moon Scorpio

Hans Christian Andersen, 2nd April 1805, Odense, Denmark, 1am, Sagittarius Ascendant, Sun in 4th, Moon Taurus

Francis Ford Coppola, 7th April 1939, Detroit, MI, USA, 1.38am, Capricorn Ascendant, Sun in 4th, Moon Scorpio

William Shatner, 22nd March 1931, Montreal, Quebec, Canada, 4am, Aquarius Ascendant, Sun in 2nd, Moon Taurus

Herbie Hancock, 12th April 1940, Chicago, IL, USA, 3.30am, Pisces Ascendant, Sun in 2nd, Moon in Gemini

Moon

Marlon Brando, 3rd April 1924, Omaha, NE, USA, 11pm, Sagittarius Ascendant, Sun in 5th, Moon Aries

Spike Milligan, 16th April 1918, Ahmadnagar, India, 2.30am, Aquarius Ascendant, Sun in 3rd, Moon Gemini

Joseph Campbell, 26th March 1904, New York, NY, USA, 7.25pm, Libra Ascendant, Sun in 6th, Moon Leo

Camille Paglia, 2nd April 1947, Endicott, New York, USA, 6.57pm, Libra Ascendant, Sun in 6th, Moon Virgo

Maya Angelou, 4th April 1928, Saint Louis, MO, USA, 2.10pm, Leo Ascendant, Sun in 8th, Moon Libra

Harry Houdini, 5th April 1874, Budapest, Hungary, 4am, Aquarius Ascendant, Sun in 2nd, Moon Scorpio

Vincent Van Gogh, 30th March 1853, Zundert, Netherlands, 11am, Cancer Ascendant, Sun in 9th, Moon Sagittarius

Al Gore, 31st March 1948, Washington, 12.53 pm, Leo Ascendant, Sun in 9th, Moon Capricorn

Kareem Abdul-Jabbar (Ferdinand Lewis Alcindor), 16th April 1947, New York, NY, USA, 6.30pm, Libra Ascendant, Sun in 7th, Moon Pisces

Houses

Lucy Lawless, 29th March 1968, Auckland, New Zealand, 6.25am, Aries Ascendant, Sun in 1st, Moon Aries

Howard Sasportas, 12th April 1948, Hartford, CT, USA, 1.46am, Capricorn Ascendant, Sun in 3rd, Moon Taurus

Dane Rudhyar, 23rd March 1895, Paris, France, 0:41am, Sagittarius Ascendant, Sun in 4th, Moon in Aquarius

William Wordsworth, 7th April 1770, Cockermouth, England, 10pm, Scorpio Ascendant, Sun in 5th, Moon Virgo

Samuel Beckett, 13th April 1906, Dublin, Ireland, 8.14pm, Scorpio Ascendant, Sun in 6th, Moon Sagittarius

Francis Ponge, 25th March 1899, Montpellier, France, 3pm, Virgo Ascendant, Sun in 8th, Moon Libra

Peter Ustinov, 16th April, 1921, London, 11am, Cancer Ascendant, Sun in 10th, Moon Leo

Gregory Peck, 5th April 1916, La Jola, CA, USA, 8am, Gemini Ascendant, Sun in 11th, Moon Taurus

Pearl Bailey, 29th March 1918, Newport News, VA, USA, 7am, Taurus Ascendant, Sun in 12th, Moon Libra

Further Information

The Astrological Association
www.astrologicalassociation.com
The Bach Centre, The Dr Edward Bach Centre, Mount Vernon,
Bakers Lane, Brightwell-cum-Sotwell, Oxon, OX10 0PZ, UK
www.bachcentre.com
Ethical Dating Site www.natural-friends.com
Mary's Home Page www.maryenglish.com

References

1. Christopher McIntosh, *Man, Myth and Magic* original: *Astrology, the Stars and Human Life: A Modern Guide*, Macdonald, London, 1970

2. Paul Sutherland, *Essentials Astronomy: A Beginner's Guide to the Sky at Night*, Igloo Books, Sywell, 2007

3. Clare Gibson, *The Astronomy Handbook: Guide to the Night Sky*, Parkham Books, Devon, 2009

4. Colin Evans, *The New Waite's Compendium of Natal Astrology, with Ephemeris for 1880–1980 and Universal Table of Houses*, Routledge & Kegan Paul, London, 1967

5. Marion D. March and Joan McEvers, *The Only Way to Learn Astrology, volume 1: Basic Principles*, ACS Publications, San Diego, CA, 1981

6. Felix Lyle and Bryan Aspland, *The Instant Astrologer*, Judy Piatkus, London, 1998

7. Caroline Casey, *Making the Gods Work for You: The Astrological Language of the Psyche*, Three Rivers Press, 1998

8. Bil Tierney, *All Around the Zodiac: Exploring Astrology's Twelve Signs*, Llewellyn Publications, USA, 2001

9. Gina Lake, *Symbols of the Soul: Discovering Your Life Purpose and Karma through Astrology*, CreateSpace Independent Publishing Platform, 2011

10. *Samuel Hahnemann, The Founder of Homoeopathic Medicine*, 'the fascinating story of the life and times of this extraordinary physician who established a system of healing which revolutionized medicine and continues to offer an effective alternative today', Thorsons Publishers, Wellingborough, 1981
    * Hahnemann's date of birth: page 15

11. Linda Goodman's search for her daughter Sarah, *The Victoria Advocate*, 27th February 1980 http://news.google.com/newspapers?id=piJIAAAAIBAJ&sjid=84AMAAAAIBAJ&pg

=7047,6190223&dq=linda+goodman&hl=en

12. Linda Goodman, *Linda Goodman's Love Signs: A New Approach to the Human Heart*, Macmillan, London, 1979

13. http://www.time.com/time/printout/0,8816,997752,00.html

Dodona Books offers a broad spectrum of divination systems to suit all, including Astrology, Tarot, Runes, Ogham, Palmistry, Dream Interpretation, Scrying, Dowsing, I Ching, Numerology, Angels and Faeries, Tasseomancy and Introspection.